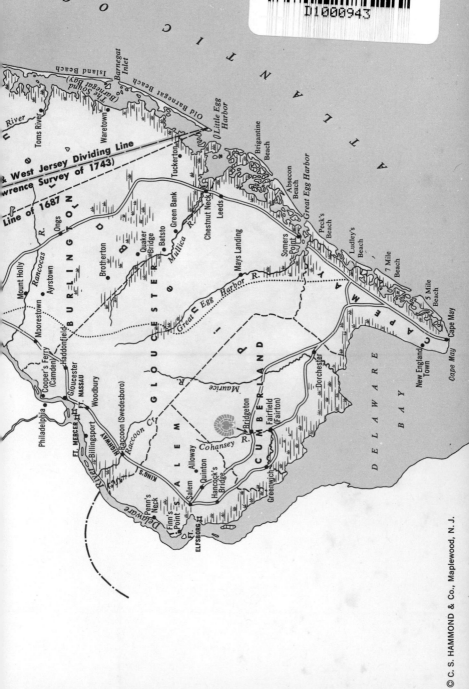

# The Story of the
# JERSEY SHORE

# THE NEW JERSEY HISTORICAL SERIES

*Edited by*

### RICHARD M. HUBER     WHEATON J. LANE

*Other books in the series will be announced*

Volume 4

The New Jersey Historical Series

# The Story of the
# JERSEY SHORE

HAROLD F. WILSON

1964

D. VAN NOSTRAND COMPANY, INC.

*Princeton, New Jersey*

*New York, N.Y. · Toronto, Canada · London, England*

D. VAN NOSTRAND COMPANY, INC.
120 Alexander St., Princeton, New Jersey (*Principal office*)
24 West 40 Street, New York 18, New York

D. VAN NOSTRAND COMPANY, LTD.
358, Kensington High Street, London, W.14, England

D. VAN NOSTRAND COMPANY (*Canada*), LTD.
25 Hollinger Road, Toronto 16, Canada

Published simultaneously in Canada by
D. VAN NOSTRAND COMPANY (Canada), LTD.

PRINTED IN THE UNITED STATES OF AMERICA

*To the students, faculty, and alumni of*

*GLASSBORO STATE COLLEGE*

who for the past 29 years have taught

a Vermonter to appreciate

NEW JERSEY

# FOREWORD

Many tracks will be left by the New Jersey Tercentenary celebration, but few will be larger than
those made by the New Jersey Historical Series.
The Series is a monumental publishing project—the
product of a remarkable collaborative effort between
public and private enterprise.

New Jersey has needed a series of books about itself.
The 300th anniversary of the State is a fitting time
to publish such a series. It is to the credit of the
State's Tercentenary Commission that this series has
been created.

In an enterprise of such scope, there must be many
contributors. Each of these must give considerably
of himself if the enterprise is to succeed. The New
Jersey Historical Series, the most ambitious publishing venture ever undertaken about a state, was conceived by a committee of Jerseymen—Julian F. Boyd,
Wesley Frank Craven, John T. Cunningham, David
S. Davies, and Richard P. McCormick. Not only did
these men outline the need for such an historic
venture; they also aided in the selection of the editors
of the series.

Both jobs were well done. The volumes speak for
themselves. The devoted and scholarly services of

Richard M. Huber and Wheaton J. Lane, the editors, are a part of every book in the series. The editors have been aided in their work by two fine assistants, Elizabeth Jackson Holland and Bertha DeGraw Miller.

To D. Van Nostrand Company, Inc. my special thanks for recognizing New Jersey's need and for bringing their skills and publishing wisdom to bear upon the printing and distributing of the New Jersey Historical Series.

RICHARD J. HUGHES
*Governor of the
State of New Jersey*

*January, 1964*

# PREFACE

The Cape Cod hook of Massachusetts, the Long Island appendix to New York, the Eastern Shore of Maryland and Virginia have all acquired special attributes that give color to their respective states. The same condition applies to the Jersey shore. "To me," said Walt Whitman in 1879, "it is the seaside region that gives stamp to Jersey."

This book covers the area of New Jersey touched by the sea, embracing the sea islands, the inlets, the bays, and the salt marshes. Here the sea has always been the shaping force. The sea islands and inlets, the bays and salt marshes were formed by its action. The islands, considered of little worth in early years, have become valuable resort sites today. The inlets, once a source of worry to early navigators as channels shifted, have become more established by protecting jetties in later years. The bays and salt marshes, so puzzling to early sailors, have become thoroughfares for small craft on the intracoastal canal.

The coast of New Jersey extends from Sandy Hook to Cape May, a distance of approximately 127 miles. For most of this distance the Atlantic Ocean beats against a low barrier of sea islands curved like a bow. All of these are separated from the mainland by what are locally called bays, channels, sounds, and salt marshes. The islands follow the entire length of the shore with two gaps. In Monmouth County from Long Branch to Point Pleasant, where certain currents have prevented the forming of barrier beaches, the projecting point of the coastal plain meets the ocean. At the southern end, the mainland again comes down to the ocean at the Cape May peninsula headland.

Despite the fact that in modern times thousands in New Jersey, New York, and Pennsylvania have become closely acquainted with the Jersey shore, the history of the region has in general passed them by. Even those who live at the shore all year around haven't had time to become deeply rooted in the region. And few of the many summer visitors stay long enough to learn anything about the influence of the past upon the present. This book is a condensation and revision of the author's *The Jersey Shore,* published in two volumes in 1953 with full footnotes. It is his hope that it will provide a readable, enlightening, and diverting experience for those who would like to know more about the Jersey shore, and the origins and development of the greatest single industry in the state: the shore resort business.

The author is grateful to the Lewis Historical Publishing Company, New York, for permission to use here illustrations from his *The Jersey Shore.* The author's special thanks are extended to the editors of the Tercentenary Series, Dr. Wheaton J. Lane and Dr. Richard M. Huber, who gave valuable advice; to Mr. James E. Downes, Mrs. Kathryn Greywacz, Mr. Robert M. Lunny, Mr. Roger H. McDonough, Mr. Harold Thompson, and Mrs. Elizabeth A. Holland, who read the manuscript and offered worthwhile suggestions; to Miss Virginia Beck, for typing the two drafts of the manuscript; to Mrs. Carol Marron, for work on the index; and to Miss Magdalena Houlroyd, Stewart Collection Curator, Glassboro State College, for assistance in search for hard-to-find material.

HAROLD F. WILSON

*Glassboro State College*
*Glassboro, New Jersey*
*February, 1964*

# TABLE OF CONTENTS

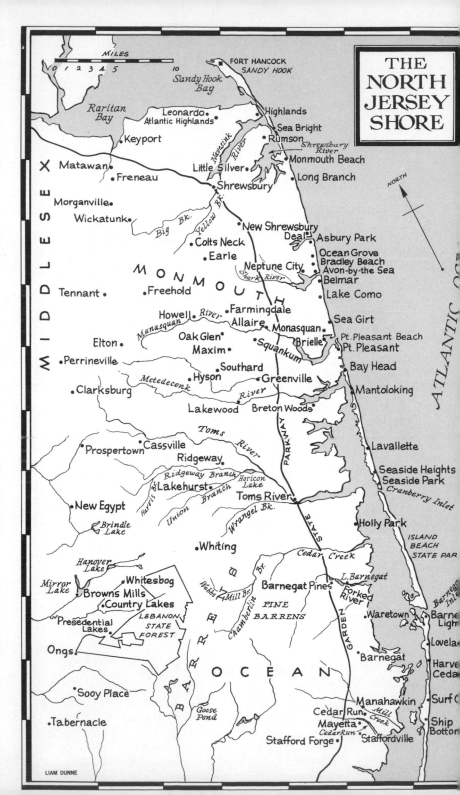

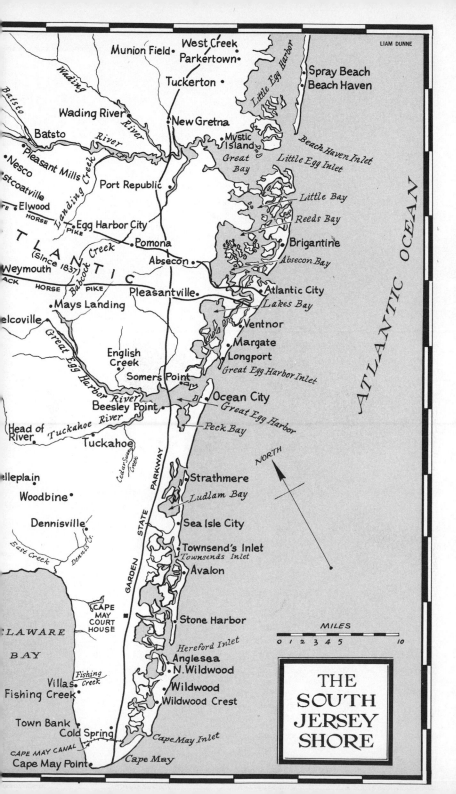

LIAM DUNNE

Munion Field • West Creek Parkertown •
Tuckerton • Spray Beach
Beach Haven

Wading River •
New Gretna •
Batsto • Mystic Island
Pleasant Mills • Great Bay
Nesco • Little Egg Inlet
tcoatville • Port Republic
Elwood • Little Bay
HORSE Egg Harbor City • Reeds Bay
PIKE Pomona • Brigantine
A T L A N T I C Absecon • Absecon Bay
(SINCE 1837)
Weymouth • Atlantic City
ACK HORSE PIKE Pleasantville • Lakes Bay
Mays Landing • Ventnor
elcoville • Margate
English Longport
Creek Great Egg Harbor Inlet
Somers Point •
Great Egg Harbor River Ocean City
Beesley Point Great Egg Harbor
Head of River
Tuckahoe River Peck Bay
Tuckahoe • NORTH
elleplain Strathmere
Woodbine • Ludlam Bay

Dennisville • Sea Isle City

Townsend's Inlet
Townsends Inlet
Avalon

CAPE
MAY Stone Harbor
COURT
HOUSE
Hereford Inlet
LAWARE Anglesea
BAY N. Wildwood
Villas • Wildwood
Fishing Creek Wildwood Crest
Town Bank
Cold Spring
CAPE MAY CANAL Cape May Inlet
Cape May Point Cape May

ATLANTIC OCEAN

MILES
0 1 2 3 4 5        10

THE
SOUTH
JERSEY
SHORE

# PART I

# THE OPENING OF THE SHORE
## 1600–1850

# I

## EARLY SHORE ACTIVITIES

> There are at least 1,200 [who] . . . came down to
> the ocean about little Egbay [Little Egg Harbor]
> and Sandy Barnegate [Barnegat] and about the
> South Cape [Cape May] there are two small kings
> with forty men apiece.
>
> A letter written in 1648

The pleasures and fruitfulness of the sea have always
enticed man to its shore. The Indians were the first summer visitors. They came down to the sea to fish and make
wampum long before Verrazano sighted this coast in
1524 and Hudson sailed north along the sea islands in
1609. The remains of their summer encampments have
left us arrowheads of jasper, cooking stones, fragments
of pottery, and piles of oyster shells. Their words are
still with us, falling musically upon the ear—Manasquan
and Mantoloking, Absecon and Tuckahoe, Manahawkin
and Metedeconk.

Few Indians were permanent residents of the actual
shore and its immediately contiguous area. What is
known about them is based on fragmentary data. One
sub-tribe of the Lenni-Lenape was called the Unalach-
tigo, signifying "People-who-live-near-the-ocean"; they
included the Absegami around Great Egg Harbor, the
Tuckahoes along the river of that name, and in the Cape
May section, the Kechemeches. Larger numbers apparently traveled from the interior to the shore for the
summer. The food from the sea offered a welcome change
in their meager diet. They relished oysters, clams, scal-

lops, whelks, sea snails, mussels, crabs, and fish. Squaws planted maize near their winter homes in May and early June, and shortly afterwards journeyed with their families to their favorite spots for the summer.

Less than a week of walking over ancient trails sufficed to bring them to the sea. They then erected temporary wigwams and proceeded to fill themselves with food from nearby water, marshes, and forests. The men went fishing and fowling, found the eggs of the marshhens and gulls, or gathered mussels and other shellfish on the mud-flats of the bays. The women tended the children, cooked the food, and gathered fuel for the circular beds of fire on which terrapin, oysters, and clams were roasted. Possessing an abundance, they began to dry the fish and oysters to take with them on their return. The main fishing points included what are now Sandy Hook, Point Pleasant, Toms River, Leeds Point, and Cape May.

Artifacts found in modern times show us the types of tools the Indians used at the shore. Fish spears have been discovered, more often in the southern section of the coastal area. Notched stones, usually called sinkers, have also been commonly found. The heavier types, crudely wrought, were used in scoop nets, gill nets, and the like; some of the smaller ones may have been used for pot lids or buttons. The large notched stones functioned as canoe anchors. Some good-sized pebbles with a hole drilled from either side may have been used in connection with nets. Celts have been unearthed in various remains. The celt was a chisel-like stone, which, when grooved on one face over the long axis, became a gouge.

Vessels of steatite, or soapstone, and of clay have been found throughout the shore area as well as potsherds or fragments of pottery. The Lenape never developed a glazed ware. The pots were used for cooking and for storage. The bottoms were nearly always egg shaped, so they could be set in holes in the sand around which a fire was built.

Along some sections of the shore, shell heaps have

been found from which fragments of pottery, stone implements, and animal bones have been unearthed. In some piles the presence of bone awls indicated that such areas were drying stations. The awls were used in stringing the dried or smoked shellfish for transportation to their winter lodges. Beneath the shell heaps skeletons of buried Indians have occasionally been found.

Some of the material in the shell piles was residue of the wampum industry. In fact one important purpose of Indian visits to the shore was to procure the raw material for wampum. In the Algonquin tribes, to which the Lenni-Lenape belonged, wampum originally meant beads made of wood. As shell wampum became more easily obtainable, the wooden was no longer used. Shell wampum was of two kinds: white and black. The white was made from the stock of the periwinkle conches, or whelks; the black from the purple inside shell of the clam. The black was considered more valuable than the white. Another variety, black on one side and mother-of-pearl on the other, was made of mussel shells. It made beautiful necklaces, but the shells were difficult to fashion.

Wampum was admired for its decorative value. Thousands of shell beads were strung on skin or sinew, and the strings made into belts in the form of sashes and scarfs or necklaces. Strings of wampum were given as an expression of sincerity in a speech, and belts as a pledge in an agreement or treaty. Unpolished wampum also was in circulation when the polished could not be obtained. The making of polished wampum was a tedious process. A quarter inch of shell was first worked into a cylindrical blank, then it was bored with a flint splinter drill, and finally it was polished for hours by hand.

After the summer at the shore, the Indians returned to their inland lodges, laden with dried and smoked oysters and clams, winkleshells for drinking cups, and large seashells for crockery. They carefully packed all the wampum they had made and put the dried and smoked fish into sacks. The squaws lashed the papooses to their shoulders and hung a string of dried fish on each arm. The men carried their tomahawks and bows and arrows, in addition to bundles of preserved wild fowl.

The first contact between Europeans and the Indians was made in September, 1609. Henry Hudson's ship, after sailing along the Jersey shore from Delaware Bay, cast anchor in Sandy Hook Bay. On September 5 some of the crew went into Newark Bay to explore. As they came back, the Indians attacked. In the fight one man, an Englishman named John Colman, was slain with an arrow in his throat. Two others were hurt. The *Half Moon* then left the Jersey shore, making its way into what is now known as the Hudson River.

Increasing encroachment by the white man during the following years gradually ended Indian visits to the shore and stimulated the removal from the State of those few who lived in the hinterland. During these years, however, the white man began a restless expansion which was to carry him westward across three thousand miles of virgin continent. As he moved into the shore areas he carefully extinguished by private deeds Indian title to land on which he planned to settle. The newcomers sometimes procured more than one Indian deed for the same property. The Indians were vague about ownership of land and boundaries. Hence, the settlers occasionally protected themselves with several deeds in return for axes, coats, kettles, pistols, wampum or "13 cases of rum, four barrels of beer, two ankers [32 gallons] of liquores." Nevertheless the paucity of the so-called Indian deeds indicates how small was the number of Indians whose claims needed to be satisfied.

The Indians failed to understand the implications of exclusive private ownership of land. The newcomers took legal possession of the land and explained the concept later. One early settler who had previously bought Sandy Hook and the lands around the Highlands from the Indians, found it necessary in 1678 to prevent their continued trespassing upon his lands. In that year he paid the Indian leader 13 shillings to relinquish his claims to hunt, fish, fowl, and gather beach plums on his domain. He gave as his reason the desire "for peace and quietness" and that for the future "I may not have any further trouble with them as formerly, . . . in their dogs killing my sheep and their hunting on my lands, and their fishing."

Action at the provincial level to gain title from the Indians came to a head in mid-eighteen century under the auspices of the Royal Colony of New Jersey. At a conference held at Crosswicks, Burlington County, in February, 1758, the Indians informed the Royal Commissioners that the lands the Indians claimed could not be described by them to persons not on the spot, as the lands were delimited by hollows and small brooks which had no certain names. They did describe certain tracts which were still claimed by individual Indians. Along the shore, these included lands from the mouth of the Metedeconk to Toms River, the area around Egg Harbor, the territory from the mouth of the Manasquan to the head of the branches, the acreage along the Shrewsbury, and the Cedar Swamp, in Cape May County near the Tuckahoe River. In return for one thousand pounds the Indians agreed to abandon their claim to any land in New Jersey not actually held by them.

The provincial Legislature decided also in 1758, to purchase a three-thousand-acre tract of land near Atsion, Burlington County, for the Indians to settle upon. The tract included a small sawmill, cedar swamp, and satisfactory hunting grounds, and some Indians moved to Edgepillick, later Brotherton, and now known as Indian Mills. This was the first Indian reservation in the country. The Government helped them get started there, by building a house of worship and several dwellings. Few Indians, however, remained on the reservation; by 1765 only 60 Indians lived there, and later the remaining few moved to New Stockbridge, the Oneida reservation in New York.

Few Indians continued to live in the shore areas. One authority estimated that as early as 1775 only about two hundred full-blooded Indians dwelt on the coastal plain of the State.

Settlements directly on the sea held little attraction for the early European arrivals. The mainland rather than the sea islands was preferred. Land inshore reached a higher value than that along the immediate coast. A Burlington Quaker, Thomas Budd, sold a large tract of land on both sides of the Great Egg Harbor River, including much of what is now Atlantic City, in the 1690's. In the sales beach lands were valued at four cents an acre and the mainland acres at ten times that amount. At Long Branch in Monmouth County, the shorefront which was to become a deciding factor in Long Branch's growth, was regarded as practically worthless by the pioneers. They sought protection from wintry gales and heavy storms by settling about a mile and a half inland.

### COLONIAL LIVELIHOODS

Samuel Smith, who wrote a history of the Colony of New Jersey published in 1765, noted there were "scattering settlements all along the coast," and listed such livelihoods as "raising cattle," the gathering of oysters "carried to New York and Philadelphia markets," and "no inconsiderable whale-fishery which might be form'd there."

The sea always conditioned the pattern of life for people who dwelt along the shore, especially in the earlier years. Later, the shore people found themselves depending for the larger part of their income on the development of the resorts, the summer trade, the convention groups, and the fishing parties. But in the colonial period, they relied to a large extent on the occupations listed by Smith, plus the making of salt.

Considerable numbers of cattle were raised on the sea islands, especially in the southern section. On an early map of Five-Mile Beach (later Wildwood), areas of timber appear, then a savanna, then a swamp, then timber, and then another savanna. The woods were thick enough to afford shelter. The same situation was true on Seven-Mile (later Avalon and Stone Harbor) and on Two-Mile Beach (later Wildwood Crest). As early as 1698, one writer declared "Cape May County, for the general part of it, is extraordinarily good and proper for the raising of all sorts of cattle, very plentiful here." About that same year, Joseph Ludlam, who had settled near Dennis, purchased what became known as Ludlam's Beach and stocked it with cattle. (Ludlam's Beach later became Strathmere and Sea Isle City.)

In colonial times cattle were identified by brands called "ear-marks," a large number of which were recorded in the county clerk's office. Branding continued throughout the period. On November 6, 1761, Aaron Leaming wrote in his diary, "Burned [branded] cattle on 5-mile beach, Nummy Island, and on 7-mile beach."

From the earliest settlement, oyster gathering offered another source of income. In fact the presence of the oyster "in great plenty and easy to take" was cited by Sir George Carteret in enumerating the advantages of the area for possible immigrants. The first settlers found oyster beds, naturally seeded, at the mouths of rivers and creeks emptying into salt-water bays and inlets. The most prolific beds were in Raritan Bay, Barnegat Bay, Little Egg Harbor, near Cape May, and the Maurice River Cove in Delaware Bay off Cumberland County.

By 1719 the General Assembly of the Province found it necessary to pass the first oyster conservation law. On March 27 of that year it was forbidden to rake or gather up oysters or shells from May 10 to September 1. This was the period when oysters would spoil before they could reach the market, the months without an "r" in them. Also the summer months were the breeding period when the oyster was small and tougher. This law also forbade non-residents to gather oysters to take away, at any time, under the penalty of forfeiting their vessel and equipment.

A familiar sight on the roads and sand-trails across the pines was the sheet-topped wagon with its ox or mule team, bringing oysters, fish, and clams from Little Egg

Harbor, Barnegat, or Absecon to the villages along the Delaware in West Jersey, or even as far as Philadelphia. For years this traffic centered around the Little Egg Harbor section, and the vehicles became known as "Egg Harbor wagons." Many of the settlers of Egg Harbor were Quakers from West Jersey and all their connections lay in that direction. From Manahawkin north the trade tended to go by sea to New York.

More colorful than the prosaic raking up of oysters, but less important as a continuing means of livelihood, was whaling. According to one authority, whaling for many turned out to be unprofitable, while the "abundance of oysters" in many localities attracted settlers. The supply of whales was eventually depleted, but the production of oysters generally increased in the nineteenth century.

The waters off the Jersey shore were considered a good hunting ground for whales. In 1633 the explorer, De Vries, then proceeding north along the coast, noted that he and his crew had speared 17 whales, but had captured only seven because of poor harpoons. Another seventeenth century chronicler, Thomas Budd, wrote in 1685 that whales were being taken off the Jersey shore from Sandy Hook to the Delaware Cape. In all probability the first white men to come to the Ocean County shores were fishermen who landed on the beach to cure their fish or to try the oil from the whales they had harpooned. The demand for whales was stimulated by the need for whale oil for lamps and whale bone for commercial uses.

Long Beach Island in Ocean County was one of the most important locations for whaling. The first claim to land on the island was granted in 1690, and in the early 1700's this was sold to Aaron Inman from New England, a whaler who raised three sons to follow that venturesome calling. Other whalers and their families later joined the Inmans. Whaling settlements, each of which had its lookout, were to be found on the island above and below what was called the "Great Swamp." Three miles north was "Harvey's Whaling Quarters," now Harvey Cedars.

The whaling in Delaware Bay resulted in the first settlement in Cape May County. Cape May Town, or Town Bank, near the point of the Cape, developed on the Delaware Bay shore for the accommodation of the whalers, a considerable number of whom came from New England and Long Island to settle permanently.

Whaling appeared to have been reasonably profitable until the time of the Revolutionary War, but following the Revolution whales grew rare off the Jersey shore, and by 1810 the industry had come to an end.

Salt production was another occupation based on the sea's bounty. Although the trade employed comparatively few shoremen, it was widely known and, during the Revolutionary War, provided the American forces with a commodity of considerable importance. Occasional efforts to derive salt from sea water, mainly for home consumption, were made before the Revolution. Clandestine establishments were constructed on the bay meadows in violation of the British mercantilist prohibitions, but did not prove financially successful. A superior product, imported from abroad, competed with the domestic product both in price and in quality. Moreover, before the Revolution, salt was obtainable from other Colonies, particularly Virginia and Massachusetts.

With the outbreak of the war, however, the production of salt along the Jersey shore boomed. No salt could come from abroad and difficulties of transportation brought about a drop in supplies from Virginia and Massachusetts. The war itself caused an increase in the demand for salt. It was needed by the patriot army not only for food but the making of gunpowder. As the war scarcity raised the price of this essential commodity, numerous evaporating works sprang up, despite the fact that labor was hard to procure. There were more alluring occupations than being sun-broiled and mosquito-bitten while tending the vats. Storms and Tories frequently destroyed the equipment, but substantial businessmen repeatedly braved the heat, insects, and poor roads to acquire salt for resale inland, where it was at some times and places as good or better than the Continental money.

Both the Continental Congress and the Province of Pennsylvania subsidized salt production along the Jersey shore. In 1778 the former constructed works on the north bank at the mouth of Toms River, and on June 24, 1776, the Pennsylvania Council of Safety voted four hundred pounds to Thomas Savadge to build similar works at Toms River. Pennsylvania also subsidized the construction of works at the mouth of Goose Creek, Barnegat Bay, a few miles from Toms River. Privately owned works included those at Forked River, Waretown, Barnegat, Little Egg Harbor, Absecon Beach, and the Friendship Works on Great Egg Harbor.

Heavy storms often caused considerable damage and impeded production. Much more serious, however, was the effect of British depredations of the defenseless Jersey coast. The English made unexpected landings at vital locations. In April, 1778, they attacked and burned the salt works established at Toms River. The works were completely rebuilt following the British departure.

The problem of securing adequate labor of the salt works became more difficult as the War continued, especially as men were called for the militia. Congress asked New Jersey not to call into service men who were employed in the salt works erected by Pennsylvania, but New Jersey replied that under her militia laws the request could not be granted. She suggested that Pennsylvania should send her own troops to carry on the works and promised to see that they were exempted, even though their residence in New Jersey would make them liable to militia service.

Some exemption was eventually allowed by the New Jersey Assembly. The majority of men employed in the works were local residents and hence subject to the State's militia call. Many petitions were sent to Governor William Livingston, and upon his recommendation the State Legislature granted exemption from militia service to "one man at each salt works for every five hundred gallons the boiling vessels held."

Following the Revolutionary War, the introduction of mined salt and its importation from abroad so reduced its price that most of the works along the coast were eventually abandoned. By 1800, salt from the Jersey shore was no longer an important staple of trade. Throughout the years of production, from the viewpoint of size of export, no wide success was obtained, but at the time when the commodity was vitally required, during the Revolution, the shore works filled a real need.

## PRIVATEERING

The thinly settled shore offered enticing opportunities for profit during the last years of the Revolution. Small villages like Toms River and Little Egg Harbor (later known as Tuckerton) found themselves receiving more and more vessels, and their streets were busy with adventurers, teamsters, and businessmen. Although salt manufacturing may have helped, the main basis for this brief flush of prosperity was privateering.

Harbors that lay behind shallow inlets through barrier beaches were conveniently close to trade routes leading to New York from the West Indies and even from Europe. These locations proved ideal retreats. The Americans were familiar with the channels, and the inlets offered a good refuge to the pursued and high hazards to the pursuers. British men-of-war might chase a privateer as far as the entrance to the passageway, but their commanders knew better than to try to follow it. Both Barnegat and Cranberry Inlets gave ready access for vessels into Barnegat Bay; the "Old Inlet" south of Long Beach did the same for small armed boats wishing to enter either Little Egg Harbor or Chestnut Neck. At the height of the privateering activity, Little Egg Harbor and Toms River were the two leading centers. The former, probably the chief base, claimed in 1778 to have about thirty armed sloops operating from it. In Cape May County the privateers based their operations mainly on the Tuckahoe River and Great Egg Harbor; in Atlantic County, at Chestnut Neck near the mouth of the Mullica River.

Some ships were especially succesful. On June 23, 1779, a small vessel called the *Skunk*, with oars for auxiliary propulsion, brought into the mouth of the Tuckahoe River at Great Egg Harbor a ship with a valuable cargo, the nineteenth prize taken since the privateer had been fitted out. Earlier in the year, the *Skunk* itself had come close to capture when it gave the gun to what appeared to be a fine prize, a good-sized vessel approaching Great Egg Harbor. After a momentary pause the merchantman was transformed into a British war vessel and in another moment she gave the *Skunk* such a broadside that, as the captain later expressed it, "The water flew around them like ten thousand whalespouts." The privateer suffered considerable damage in her sails and rigging, but by hard rowing made good her escape.

Vessels and their contents were usually sold at public auction and the proceeds divided among the privateersmen. Interest in the size of the shares was avid, and it sometimes seemed that the people along the shore were negligent of everything but dividing and detemining their shares in prizes. A typical sale which occurred at Great Egg Harbor was advertised in the *Pennsylvania Packet* of Philadelphia, on March 11, 1777; it gave notice:

the brigantine, the "Defiance," with all her tackle, apparel and furniture, now lying at the mouth of Tuckahoe River in Great Egg Harbor Inlet, and the cargo . . . consisting of molasses, sugar, coffee, cocoa, salt, cotton, etc., and sundry whaling tackle [would be sold at public vendue] at the house of a John Somers, jun., on the 12 instant, cash to be paid on the delivery of the goods.

Not all the privateersmen using the harbors were Jerseymen. The *New Jersey Gazette* for August 5, 1778, announced, "Lately brought into Little Egg Harbor by two New England privateers . . . a brig and a sloop loaded."

The same issue carried the story of a sloop from Jamaica, bound for New York, that was brought into Little Egg Harbor by a number of Americans. This group had been captured at sea, landed at Jamaica, and were being transported to New York as prisoners. As they voyaged north up the Jersey coast, they overpowered the crew, took possession of the vessel, and brought it in as a prize. The cargo was a valuable one, consisting of rum, sugar, and other Jamaican products.

Two privateersmen, both from New Brunswick, became especially well known along the shore for their exploits. The venturesome Captain William Marriner took nine men out in a large boat into Raritan Bay and recaptured the onetime privateer, *Blacksnake*. With this vessel, he put to sea for prizes. He met off Long Beach Island the British *Morning Star* which carried six swivel guns and 33 men, which he captured after killing three of her crew and wounding five. He then ran both prizes into Little Egg Harbor.

Captain Adam Hyler, mainly operating in the Raritan Bay and the Sandy Hook area, frequently sailed off Long Beach Island. He generally depended upon whale boats or large barges, rowed by skilled crews of a dozen or more men, selected for their endurance and courage. The members of his crew were taught to be expert at the oar and to row silently. According to a contemporary report, his captures were made chiefly by surprise or strategem. In one instance, the captain of one of the captured vessels himself related that on a peaceful, moonlit night he was on deck with three or four men, with his vessel at anchor near Sandy Hook, and the man-of-war, *Lion,* about a quarter of a mile distant. Suddenly the group heard several pistols discharged into the cabin and turned to find at their elbows a number of armed men, who, according to the captain:

had fallen as it were from the clouds, who ordered us to "surrender" in a moment or we were "dead men." Upon this, we were turned into the hold and the hatches barred over us. The firing, however, had alarmed the man-of-war, who hailed us and desired to know what was the matter. As we were not in a situation to answer, at least so far as to be heard, Captain Hyler was kind enough to do so for us, telling them through the speaking trumpet that "all was well," after which, unfortunately, they made no further inquiry.

One of the larger centers for privateering was Toms River, which used Cranberry Inlet. In 1778, an English ship from Bristol ran ashore near the inlet. The militia seized the valuable cargo, refloated the vessel, brought her inside the inlet and into Toms River. The Court of Admiralty ordered, from Trenton, a portion of the cargo sold at Toms River, consisting of "Bristol beer, cider, porter, salt, flour, cheese, red and white wine, queen's and delft ware, wine glasses, tumblers, etc." Later, the rest of the cargo was sold at Manasquan.

The seized vessel was renamed the *Washington* and armed as a privateer, anchoring in Barnegat Bay just inside the inlet. A few days later, two British men-of-war and two brigs appeared off the inlet and lay there all night. Early next morning, in seven armed boats, they pushed through the passageway and retook the ship along with two sloops that were lying alongside. Some of the crew escaped.

The British endeavored to destroy the privateers' harbors, those "nests of pirates." Every royal man-of-war passing along the shore tried to capture or destroy whatever craft, peaceable or predatory, it might find heading from one of the inlets. The major planned offensive took place in October, 1778, when the neighboring hamlets of Chestnut Neck, on the south side of the Mullica, Bass River on the north side, and Little Egg Harbor were attacked from the sea.

At Chestnut Neck wagonmen had a thriving business going. They hauled to points on the Delaware the valuables captured and brought into the refuge. To protect the place from possible British attack from New York, authorities built a small fort and purchased a number of cannon. Earlier in 1778, when the British were in possession of Philadelphia and Washington's battered army was in Valley Forge, supplies had been brought into the harbor of Chestnut Neck in small vessels from the South and conveyed by wagon train across the State to the Continental army at Valley Forge. Furthermore, up the river above Chestnut Neck, at Batsto, cannon balls were being moulded of bog iron for use in the American army.

The British hoped to raze this small production center. An expedition, consisting of the flagship, the frigate *Zebra,* plus three sloops, two galleys, and four armed boats, manned by 300 soldiers and 100 New Jersey Loyalists, left New York the last day of September, 1778. High winds prevented them from getting their larger ships over the shoals of the Old Inlet. The leader then filled his galleys and armed boats with men and started through the Great Bay–Mullica River passage, toward Chestnut Neck on the south side of the river. The British charged the breastworks there, and thanks to the covering fire from the galleys, forced the American militia to retreat. The British then burned 30 vessels, including eight sloops and schooners, and more large whaleboats. The village was burned, along with the storehouse on the wharf, and the breastworks were destroyed. After burning a salt works across the Mullica River, and a few more houses near the mouth of Bass River, the British returned to Chestnut Neck anchorage where they found the *Zebra* aground on the bar at the entrance of the inlet. The following days they burned farms and vessels at the mouth of the Wading River, which flows into the Mullica. Rebuffed in their move toward Batsto, they headed toward Little Egg Harbor. General Pulaski, dispatched by Washington, arrived too late to save its outskirts, but now that the countryside was aroused and Pulaski's troops were nearby, the British retired to Chestnut Neck and headed for the inlet and the open sea. The *Zebra,* which had been refloated, again ran aground and was fired by the British to prevent her from falling into the hands of the patriots. Within a short time, Little Egg Harbor resumed its privateering activities.

An attack on Toms River occurred four years later, in 1782, when the war was nearly over. Cornwallis had surrendered at Yorktown, but the Treaty of Peace had not yet been signed. The expedition was instigated, to a considerable extent, by the Board of Associated Royalists, presided over by William Franklin, Tory son of the famed Benjamin and last Royal Governor of New Jersey. He was determined to wipe out the rebel town which had so long been a rendezvous for privateers.

In March, 1782, the British expedition, composed of about forty "Refugee Loyalists" and eighty British troops, passed through Cranberry Inlet in armed whaleboats during the night, and early in the morning attacked the Toms River blockhouse, defended by twenty-five men under Captain Joshua Huddy. Soon the American ammunition gave out, and in the British assault nine patriots were killed and twelve made prisoner. Three British soldiers were killed. Toms River village now lay open and more than a dozen houses, a gristmill, and a sawmill were burned. The large barge owned by that famous privateersman Captain Hyler was seized and taken away, along with other craft. Among the prisoners taken was Captain Huddy; he was subsequently hanged by the British at the Highlands in Monmouth County. The signing of the Treaty of Peace at Paris put an end to British retaliatory expeditions against the Jersey shore, and, with the turn of the century, the first resorts began to emerge along the coast.

# II

# THE FIRST RESORTS

---

Sometimes, in early July, daily about noon . . .
(there) might be seen ten to twelve stages filled
mostly with ladies whose happy faces, quiet de-
meanor, and sombre garb, told you that they were
from the Quaker City and that after a rest in
Rice's Hotel [in Freehold] they would be on their
way to Long Branch for the season.

Monmouth County observer of the 1840's

Between 1800 and 1850 New Jersey's first seaside resorts
developed. There were Cape May and Long Branch, and
to a lesser extent, Tucker's Beach and Long Beach. A
number of other places were entertaining a few summer
guests, though they were too small to be termed resorts.
This last category included the settlements described
by Gordon in his 1834 *Gazetteer* as having boarding
houses, such as Somers Point or Manasquan.

Before the railroads came, vacationers had only two
means of getting to the seashore. One was the overland
route, which necessitated a long and difficult journey
through the pine belt by wagon and later by stagecoach
from either Philadelphia or New York. This method
was most frequently employed to reach the central section of the shore, including what became Ocean County
and Atlantic County. The other was the water route to
Cape May and to Long Branch. Cape May was patronized
principally by Philadelphians and Southerners. In the
early part of this period Long Branch was visited mainly
by Philadelphians by stagecoach, but later many people
from New York came by boat.

Before the stagecoach lines developed, the overland route to the shore relied on makeshift arrangements. The trip was often made in freight wagons, known as "Jersey wagons" or "oyster wagons." Another name for this type of vehicle was "shore wagon." Traders carted salted fish and oysters from Little Egg Harbor through the pines to Philadelphia and Trenton in the later eighteenth and nineteenth centuries. On their return trips, they brought back visitors to the shore, who, before boarding houses were established, carried with them their stoves, blankets, and food. Women seldom traveled by wagon, as the trip was considered too long and too rough for females.

## BY LAND AND BY SEA

Let those who now comfortably drive down to the seashore in automobiles recall what it was like over one hundred years ago. "Of all wheeled vehicles, the greatest atrocity was this Jersey wagon," declared one resident as he recalled jouncing trips to the shore in the 1830's and 1840's. "It seemed to have been designed by the Shakers in protest against every semblance of luxury or even comfort." The back and sides were square, straight, and "as free from graceful lines as those of a ready-made coffin." The springs were "cumbrous contrivances of unyielding wood so constructed as to make riding a weariness to the flesh and the spirit." Insect pests added to the travelers' discomfort. When the passengers stopped for meals, voracious green-head flies made "one continuous meal" off them. By the time they reached their destination "the more robust were generally able to climb out but the feebler ones . . . had to be lifted out."

The stagecoach was a real improvement over the Jersey wagon. The coach left Camden at four o'clock in the morning and got to Cape May after midnight, a hard trip of about one hundred and ten miles. The first stage between Philadelphia and Tuckerton was established in 1816. One round trip a week was made. It took two days to travel each way, and the horses were allowed to rest a day. Visitors were transported by boat from Tuckerton across the bay to Tucker's Beach and to Long Beach. By 1833 access to Long Beach had been improved. An excursion was recommended that year to the resort, "opposite the little village of Manahawkin," to which "a good stage with four horses runs every Monday, Wednesday, and Friday from Burlington."

Lines to Absecon and to Leeds Point were available for Atlantic County (which had been part of Gloucester County until 1837). For Beesleys Point on Great Egg Harbor, in northern Cape May County, passengers took the Tuckahoe stage leaving Philadelphia every Tuesday, Thursday, and Saturday morning. No steamboat connections developed for the central shore points, and when railroad facilities became available there was no need for them.

Travel by boat to the vicinity of Cape May was less taxing. Although sporadic service started earlier, it was not until 1802 that vessels using sails and carrying freight and passengers were running regularly during the season between Philadelphia and Cape May. In 1815 a sailing sloop was especially constructed to bring people down the Delaware from Philadelphia. The trip usually took two days under sail. By the end of the first quarter of the century the first steamboat began to ply between the two places. An account of a trip to Cape May in 1823 exclaims,

Behold us pushed off from the wharf [at Philadelphia], with about 80 passengers. . . . What elegance in this vessel! How rapidly the passed objects fade from view! . . . We reach the Cape at six o'clock. As we near the beach [Delaware Bay side] we see many carriages in waiting to bear us to the boarding-houses three miles on the opposite sea beach. . . .

Boats for Cape May stopped at Newcastle, Delaware, to take on Baltimoreans and visitors from the South.

In the next period, the route to Long Branch was considerably improved. Faster and more comfortable accommodations became available. By 1825 many travelers took a steamboat up to Bordentown on the Delaware, where they found good stage connections to Long Branch. At the height of the season, from twenty-eight to thirty stages regularly used this route.

The development of water transportation from New York to Long Branch increased its patronage. For a number of years New Yorkers reached the place by taking a ship to Red Bank on the North Shrewsbury River, then a six-mile stage to Long Branch. Later a steamboat company inaugurated service between New York and Sandy Hook, where stages from Long Branch, "odd, wide-wheeled beach wagons," carried New York passengers on the slow, hot drive down the sea island to the resort. Sixty stagecoaches were frequently lined up to convey passengers down the beach road to Long Branch. Still later, steamboats landed just inside Old Shrewsbury Inlet. The boat trip from New York to the Inlet, travelers agreed, was likely to be more comfortable, but the road from there down the beach to Long Branch was so sandy that meadow grass had to be spread over the ruts to prevent the eight-inch wide wheels from sinking to their hubs. Boats did not dock directly at Long Branch until 1828.

### BOARDING HOUSE LIFE

Once at the shore visitors stayed in farm houses which took in a few guests, or in the boarding houses which were scattered along the coast. Conveniences were few, but the rates were comparatively low. At one on Long Beach Island from four to five dollars a week was charged for board and room, and twenty-five cents a day paid for boat and bait for fishing and crabbing. Proprietors made a specialty of feeding their guests on chicken, fish, and oysters. The chicken and fish were served at regular meals, and the oysters were to be found in a heap under the shed where the boarders were free to go and eat as many as they chose to open.

Life at the boarding houses tempted description. Cape

May was pictured by one observer in 1823 as a village of about twenty houses with clean and grassy streets. He added in a disappointed tone that time often passed slowly for the guests. They had to provide their own amusements. "Last night," he wrote, "one of the gentlemen played tunes on his flute and several made themselves merry with dancing in the dining hall." A number of his fellow lodgers who had stayed out their time were expressing much desire to see the steamboat again to take them home. The semi-weekly turnover of guests offered excitement, even though it brought inconveniences. The arrival of the new company and the departure of some of the old twice a week produced a great bustle, since for one night both parties remained in the house and several gentlemen were usually left to take their rest on tables, chairs, and settees.

No reservations were made in advance, and crowded conditions often resulted. A visitor who went to Absecon Beach by stagecoach in 1843 explained that his group went to Andrew Leeds' boarding house, where they were shown to a room ten by twelve feet. Four of them were to occupy it. The house was already full of boarders and the proprietor was not eager to accommodate them. As it is today, the weather was of first importance. The first day of their visit it stormed all day, and their spirits were low. On the next day they were able to go in the surf for a while, but the writer complained of the ravenous mosquitoes. After tea they formed a cotillion, partly to amuse themselves, but more for the purpose of ridding themselves of those "consining insects." Soon they were asked to discontinue by the landlady who said her neighbors might be disturbed and complain, though the nearest house was a mile and a half away. She then added she did not think it "a very moral recreation." On the following day the group took a walk along the beach but were bothered by swarms of mosquitoes. "We decided to leave the following morning," the commentator concluded succinctly.

Boarding-house life at Long Beach in those decades

had its disadvantages, although the visitors did not expect the comforts of home.

In the 1820's travelers to Long Beach usually went from Philadelphia by stage to Tuckerton and by boat the next day over to Long Beach. The boat fare was twenty-five cents. One popular hostelry was Horner's Boarding House, built by Philadelphians for the pleasure of "sea-bathing." One guest recalled in 1823 that this boarding house was made for good cheer and free and easy comforts without any attempt at elegance. None of the floors were planed and the side walls were rough boards and the ceilings white-washed. But the liquor and food were good. The bathers had to walk half a mile to the shore across the sand, and the ladies rode in a cart to get to the surf. As there were fine shooting and fishing and good surf, Long Beach was popular with men who liked a rough and vigorous outdoor life.

Even in these decades there was a flourish of holiday gaiety in the boarding houses, which often aroused some muttering criticisms in the more dour vacationers. The guests felt a relaxation from all the usual cares of housekeeping or business, and some behaved in an uninhibited manner. This was often deeply distressing to the more sedate patrons. A summer visitor at a boarding house in Cape May in 1823 referred to it as a "sans souci" establishment. He described the arrival of ten new guests, chiefly Quaker ladies, who came by steamboat in the late afternoon. Soon afterward a company of 15 men and five women, from Cape Henlopen in Delaware, burst in to have supper and spend the night, "freed from the concerns and obligations of life." This group had a fiddler and considerable to drink. After supper they "set to dancing and rude mirth and kept it up boisterously until midnight." The Quaker ladies were not amused.

The same distinction at holiday resorts then between the sedate and the gay was not so different from what it is now. In the 1840's, at Ryan's Boarding House at Absecon Beach, one observer described an occasion when many of the guests went down to the beach and danced "to the strains of Fisher's hornpipe discoursed by a single fiddle . . . a regular jump-up-and-down, cross-over-Jonathan, and figure-in-Jemina terpsichorean fling!" At high tide they bathed. The hilarity of the occasion mounted to a crescendo when the men carried the "blushing and screaming maidens" to the tops of the steep sand hills and tying their feet together, rolled them down to the water's edge. There were no bathhouses and the guests went among the dunes to change into their bathing clothes.

Long Beach, too, had its "gay lifers." At the lower end of the beach, it was recalled, practical jokers were very busy. One of their oft-repeated pranks was to requisition the hotel mule and in a personally conducted tour lead him up and down the bare floors of the halls without regard to the sleep of the other guests. A proprietor returned to his establishment once to find a favorite cow marooned on the third floor. It took some time and effort to get the animal back to the ground.

## HOTELS, AMERICAN PLAN

By mid-nineteenth century larger establishments which could be regarded as hotels had been built in many places. By 1834, according to the State *Gazetteer,* there were in Cape May six boarding houses, three of them large. Cape May was the first of the resorts to build hotels. In 1832 the "Mansion House" was constructed with laths and plaster. The Census of 1840 revealed that Cape Island then had two large hotels, and a third was in the process of erection. This was four stories high and a hundred feet long. Two more had been built by mid-century.

By 1805 there were accommodations on the beach at Long Branch, as well as in the old village of the same name which was not on the ocean. One New Yorker recorded in that year that there were on the beach three large frame buildings or boarding houses, each capable of entertaining a hundred boarders. Considering that the season lasted but three months, the terms for board, eight dollars per week, appeared to him to be very reasonable.

The boarding houses continued their ascendancy through the 1830's and into the first years of the 1840's. In the forties, however, the modest farmhouses and small frame dwellings used as boarding houses at Long Branch were being replaced by more imposing structures called "houses" and later hotels. One, built in 1839, accommodated 175 guests. Another hotel appeared in 1846 called the Allegheny House, the largest of its time. Like most of its predecessors it was a remodeled farmhouse. This was the first step toward the introduction of luxury hotels at Long Branch, but it was not until the period following 1850 that hotels reached their peaks in purveying "elegant hospitalities."

## WATERY JOY

The *pièce de résistance* of a vacation at the shore was, of course, "sea-bathing." This pastime was considered of sufficient attraction to be used as a headline in an advertisement of the Philadelphia and Absecombe Accommodation Line of Stages in 1835, and a few decades later it was referred to as "the principal amusement," with "no end of watery joy till the dinner bell rings."

Throughout the nineteenth century people went in bathing and not in swimming. Thanks to the type of bathing suit then in vogue, swimming was a most difficult form of exercise. "Sea-bathing" consisted of wading in the water and jumping joyously up and down in the surf. An advertisement for Cape May appearing in a Philadelphia paper in 1801 stated that Cape May was a good place to visit for those "who use sea-bathing; . . . the shape of the shore is so regular that persons may wade a great distance." The ladies did not venture very far into the water. A Cape May visitor describing the sea-bathing in 1823 observed that the ladies wore flannel and other woolen dresses, and that none went in the water beyond half their height.

In many resorts, mixed bathing was frowned upon in the early years of the century, although no vigorous measures to prevent it were taken. "In order to prevent intrusion," read a sign at the Mansion House in Cape May in 1839, "a white Flag will be on the Bath House during the Ladies' hours and a red Flag for the Gentlemen." This same sign also announced regulations concerning guests. At the table, the new guest was to take his seat at the foot when he arrived and was allowed to advance to the head as others left. Guests were warned that the house closed at half-past ten in the evening. Breakfast was at half-past seven, dinner at two o'clock, supper at half-past six. A bell was rung half an hour before meals. For baths inside the hotel, special times were reserved, since there were no rooms with private baths in those days. The sign stated: "Bathing Hours: In the Forenoon, Gentlemen until 6 o'clock, Ladies from 6 to 7 and from 11 to 12. Afternoon: Ladies $4\frac{1}{2}$ – $5\frac{1}{2}$, Gentlemen $5\frac{1}{2}$ – $6\frac{1}{2}$."

During the season at Cape May, it was the custom for girls to go into the sea with flowing locks, regardless of the damage the water might do. It was said that the popularity of a girl was measured by the number of men who asked to dry her hair. In fact, the most admired ones let men either "cut in" on the drying or "take turns."

Other than the "sea-bath," there were few opportunities for recreation. A commentator explained in 1823:

Among our few amusements, . . . we swim; gather curious shells and pebbles upon the strand; walk the piazza and converse. A curious and laughable exercise is to try to walk blindfolded to any given object in a direct line. Ladies and gentlemen exercise at this. Some pitch quoits; some play domino. We go out to see the drawing of the seine about one-sixth of a mile from shore.

In the eyes of many guests, one of the most thrilling diversions at Cape May was the chance to see in the flesh all the distinguished visitors. This was true to some extent in the 1840's, although more famous people "seasoned" at Cape May in the decades following 1850.

It is probable that no other visitor in the 1840's caused such great excitement as did Henry Clay, who was a guest at the Mansion House for a week during the summer of 1847. He came to Cape May to rest following the death of his son in a battle in the Mexican War. Although Clay had been defeated in the presidential campaign of 1844, he was still highly popular. It was recounted that he liked "sea-bathing" and bathed twice a day, but that he had lost much of his hair to souvenir hunters! (These were the days when the making of hair wreaths was popular.) The ladies caught him and with a pair of scissors carried for just that purpose clipped locks from his head to remember him by.

Gradually Cape May began to emerge as a major resort on the Jersey shore. A survey published in 1844 called it "a favorite watering place." It had in all about fifty dwellings. In the summer the resort was described as being thronged with visitors, principally from Philadelphia; it was estimated that three thousand came annually. Southern planters, cotton, sugar, and tobacco brokers, and Southern statesmen and their families also found the gay life to their liking.

Visitors, mainly from Philadelphia, also went to Tucker's Beach and Long Beach, in what became Ocean County, which was separated from Monmouth County in 1850. In fact, these two places were among the earliest of summer resorts. About 1765 Reuben Tucker, who had bought the whole island south of Long Beach in 1745, opened his home for the "health and entertainment of pleasure seekers." His boarding house became well known and was still in business in 1823. On the southern end of Long Beach, the first house, built about 1815, was sold in 1822 to a group of Philadelphia men who had been patronizing it for summer outings. They enlarged it in 1823. About twelve miles north of Tucker's Beach was another boarding house called the "Mansion of Health." It was built in 1822 near what was then known as the "Great Swamp," near present-day Surf City. The house was 120 feet long and located a tenth of a mile from the sea. For that distance, however, the few lady guests were provided with an ox-wagon to get to the surf and to ride along the beach, "wherein they amuse themselves greatly in a rustic novel way." Near by was the house owned by the Inmans, which was the center of considerable whaling activity in earlier days. For many years whale bones "lying about bleaching in the sun" attracted the curiosity of visitors.

By 1848 Harvey Cedars, still further north on the island, had a boarding house to which groups of young Philadelphians went on brief two- or three-day excursions. The young men in the party shared expenses. The main attraction there, in addition to the usual sea-bathing, was a series of dances held in an adjacent hall. Three locally celebrated fiddlers furnished the music, one of whom, it was said, could play any tune after hearing it once and would also reel off his own compositions by the score. There was a raised platform for the fiddlers at the south end of the hall and from here the dances would be "called."

Long Branch in Monmouth County had numerous opportunities for recreation. Wrote "Amicus" in the *New York Herald*, after visiting the resort in 1805:

I am a friend to innocent and reasonable amusements, many of which the visitors to Long Branch already have: viz.: the sedentary or serious enjoy riding, walking, reading, social converse—a cheerful cigar and a half pint of wine after dinner; the young and gay have dancing and tea parties, excursions to the neighboring villages; and lately horse racing has been introduced which, by the way, I don't like much, but hope it will be hereafter on the . . . plan where there is to be no gaming,

a hope, however, which was not fulfilled.

The sea was always the lure that drew people to the resort. As in Cape May, efforts were made to prevent mixed bathing. Unmarried men and girls did not bathe together. On the bluff just south of what became Broadway, where stairs later descended to the beach, a flag was raised to announce which sex then had the privilege of using the beach. Again as in Cape May, a white flag was the signal for the women, a red for the men. Husbands, however, could accompany their wives when the white flag was up. An unwritten law forbade women from appearing on the beach before six in the morning, for prior to that hour, according to a guidebook published later, "the gentlemen had the only privilege of disporting themselves in natural abandon." Apparently the women were early risers themselves, for another periodical assured the reader that the ladies were so far back from the beach at their boarding houses that the bluffs adequately concealed the early morning bathers.

Life at Long Branch particularly was taken seriously by those who came to the beach in these earlier years. The resort was described in the 1820's as a sedate watering place with grace said at each meal, hymns sung in the evening, and prayer meetings held regularly. The visitors enjoyed simple pleasures. They promenaded along Ocean Avenue, which was then a narrow wagon track with only six buildings along it. They collected shells and varicolored pebbles. Ladies were fond of drying starfish, which they wore suspended from satin ribbons. Amateur art flourished in the form of round cheesebox covers, wooden shovels, and even rolling pins decorated with colorful seascapes. These articles were packed up at the close of the visit and removed to the city to adorn parlor walls. It was recounted that yards and yards of dark green seaweed were often draped over curtain poles to serve as portieres. Fishnets were also sometimes used for the same purpose.

By the 1830's, however, the place had begun to assume a gayer air. Card playing, billiards, bowling, dancing, and faster driving on the beach gradually became more familiar sights, although these new pastimes drew the fire of the traditionalists. One observer, referring to this new spirit of restlessness, blamed it on the wives; he had nothing but pity, he said, for the husbands who "stalk gloomily about, catching one meal here and another there."

Long Branch had fewer famous visitors prior to 1850 than did Cape May. The place gained considerable publicity, however, from Mrs. Frances Trollope, the famous English commentator. Even though she did not get to the resort in her "snoopy peregrinations" over America in 1830, she provided advocates of Long Branch with something to talk about. When she reached Philadelphia that summer she found that many of the best families had left for Long Branch. When she heard of the bathing customs there, she wrote she was amazed that the ladies did not follow the English practice of being wheeled into the water in bathing machines, a kind of portable bathhouse in which they undressed and dressed. Mrs. Trollope did acknowledge the propriety of one custom which she heard was followed at Long Branch. When ladies at their boarding houses asked gentlemen to accompany them "to taste the briny wave," two ladies always invited one jointly, for, she added, "custom does not authorize a tête-à-tête immersion."

By 1850 the resort industry was established on the Jersey shore. But during the first half of the century, the lives of shore residents were affected by influences more serious than the development of recreation facilities.

# III

# WAR, SHIPBUILDING
# AND SHIPWRECKS

---

While the barges were at the [Barnegat] inlet, a
party landed on the beach, . . . and killed fifteen
head of cattle. The British left word that if the
owners presented a bill to Commodore Hardy,
he would settle it. But the owners were too patri-
otic to attempt anything that seemed like furnish-
ing supplies to the enemy.

Account of event on Long Beach Island, 1813

In the middle Atlantic states there was little enthusiasm
for a declaration of war against Great Britain in 1812.
This was particularly true on the New Jersey shore where
the Quaker influence was strong, as in Shrewsbury, Tuckerton, the Somers Point area, and the northern part of
Cape May County. War was declared by the United
States on June 19, 1812. Two months earlier State
militia men had been posted along the coast to protect
the State against possible invasion. Five companies of
infantry and one of artillery, for example, were stationed
for a short time at Navesink Highlands. Egg Harbor
Township formed a militia company to man a small fort
at Great Egg Harbor, on the parapet of which were
mounted four- and six-pound cannon, sufficient protection against most wooden vessels. The fort was never
attacked.

Attempts to form local militia often proved unsuc-
cessful, since many of the men were already involved

in sea service. Efforts were then made to draft men. The militia officers, however, allowed the draftees to procure substitutes on payment of a bounty of fifty dollars, a forerunner of the vicious custom prevalent during Civil War conscription. In the dune village on Long Beach Island one man in every seven was called to help protect the coast. The men clubbed together and hired substitutes. The County militia was later sent to help man the fortifications at Sandy Hook, guarding the approach to New York harbor.

Sandy Hook was a favorite cruising ground for British ships blockading the port of New York. The vessels frequently entered Sandy Hook Bay itself, and some were seized by daring American sailors. One of the most notable of these captures was made off Sandy Hook by a fishing smack, the *Mad Jack Percival,* which in celebration of the Fourth of July, 1813, sailed boldly out into the Bay. A calf, a sheep, and a goose had been secured to the deck of the vessel, and 30 men, well armed, were secreted in the cabin and forepeak. Three men on deck were dressed in fisherman's apparel. The British sloop *Eagle* gave chase. On overhauling it and finding there was livestock aboard, the *Eagle* ordered the little ship to report to the commodore of a British man-of-war five miles distant. The helmsman of the smack answered "Aye, aye, sir!" and turned the helm. This brought him alongside the *Eagle,* not three yards away. The Americans then rushed on deck from their hiding places and poured into the *Eagle* a volley that drove the latter's crew so precipitously into the hold that they did not have time to strike the flag. Three of the British were killed in the attack. There were no casualties among the Americans. The *Eagle* was brought to the Battery in New York in the afternoon, and the prisoners were landed amid the thousands of Americans assembled at the Battery to celebrate the anniversary of Independence.

In what became Ocean County the residents were subjected during the war to raids and seizures. A number of coastal vessels were caught and burned by the British. The English blockaders often sent a barge ashore at some point on the coast to kill and dress cattle on the sea islands and take the beef back to the ship. One incident that aroused the populace occurred in early 1813 when a 74-gun British ship lay off Barnegat Inlet waiting for American vessels that might try to slip through the blockade. The Commodore sent barges with armed men into the shallow inlet. Once through, they boarded a schooner and attempted to take it out, but ran it aground. Thereupon they set fire to it and its cargo of lumber. They then seized a sloop laden with lumber and supplies, fired it, and hurried back. The attack had been witnessed from the nearby Waretown shore, where the citizens became greatly alarmed since they had heard of the plundering expeditions under Admiral Cockburn on the Virginia and Maryland shores. The women and children were sent into the woods for safety, and the men out to the sloop to extinguish the fire. At nearby Forked River, people stood on the roofs of houses and watched the events inside the inlet.

Cape May residents felt the presence of war in a number of ways. On the bay shore many people fared badly in the loss of cattle and other possessions which could be carried away. Vessels at Fishing Creek were destroyed by fire in British forays. A sloop was burned and the crew and passengers, among whom were two sisters coming home from Philadelphia, were taken prisoners. The Fishing Creek salt works were destroyed. On the sea side of the County, frequent landings were made on the islands to kill cattle for beef.

Some coastal privateering occurred during the War, although much less than in the Revolution when more prizes were available nearby. In the War of 1812, the British blockade was tighter. Privateers still used the inlets, particularly Barnegat (since Cranberry Inlet had closed in since the Revolution) and a new one which had opened through Tucker's Beach in 1800.

Long before the War of 1812 and even before the Revolution, shipbuilding had developed along the Jersey coast. Whaleboats were built before 1700, while various types of fishing boats were produced almost from the beginning of European occupancy of the coast. The clumsy scow and the "garvey" were constructed so simply that any house carpenter could build them. The garvey was long in use for oystering and clamming; in fact, it is still popular in Barnegat Bay for sport fishing. The scow transported salt hay from marshes to farm. By 1790 Tuckerton, Forked River, Barnegat, and Toms River were busy constructing coasting vessels, the size of which had gradually increased to eight hundred tons.

A larger proportion of the residents of Atlantic and Ocean Counties depended upon shipbuilding for a livelihood than in the other shore counties where more varied industries were undertaken. By 1800 Tuckerton had as many as five brigs under construction at once in one shipyard. Ebenezer Tucker, the Pharos, the Bartletts, and other men of Tuckerton put out vessel after vessel. The industry also flourished at Waretown, Forked River, Barnegat, and Toms River in the first quarter of the century. In Atlantic County by 1850, according to the Census, shipbuilding was the leading "mechanical business," principally conducted at Absecon, Bakersville, Leedsville, Mays Landing, Tuckahoe, and Port Republic, while agricultural pursuits were "quite limited." In all these towns the small schooner was the favorite, being especially fitted for the lumber, cordwood, and charcoal trade from the interior.

One of the most notable builders of his day was Joseph Francis of Toms River. He constructed a rowboat in 1830 which was later presented to the Russian Czar, who used it at the Cowes Regatta in England. Later, Francis designed and built a wooden lifeboat patterned after the whaleboat, but which afforded greater buoyancy and stability due to masses of cork fixed in the bow and stern and air chambers laid along the gunwales and under the thwarts. In 1843 he built the first corrugated metal life-boat and later formed a company for its manufacture in Brooklyn. It was there that he invented the life-car described at the end of this chapter. Congress later gave him, in the words of a regional historian, "the most massive gold medal ever awarded by that body to any individual," which Francis afterward presented to the Smithsonian Institution.

Mays Landing, at the head of navigation of the Great Egg Harbor River, became the center of ship-building in Atlantic County. The town had been founded by George May in mid-eighteenth-century, when he opened a store to supply the vessels putting into Great Egg Harbor. George May was a blacksmith and a ship-builder as well; he built a number of schooners, many for the West Indies trade. In the fifty years from 1830, more than a hundred vessels were built in Mays Land-ing, with lumber from nearby forests and iron from the local foundries.

In Cape May County shipbuilding was centered at Tuckahoe and Dennisville. Tuckahoe builders took advantage of the white cedar in the Great Cedar Swamp and the nearby bog-iron ore furnaces. In the 1820's, blacksmiths journeyed up the river from Tuckahoe to Etna Furnace for bar iron to make spikes and bolts for the vessels on the stocks. The spikes were six inches to two feet in length to suit the various thicknesses of ship timber. Dennisville produced still more craft, and by mid-century shipbuilding was conducted there on a large scale.

In Monmouth County one of the earliest shipbuilding centers was at Red Bank on the Navesink River, where vessels were constructed for the Monmouth County–New York trade. By 1809 *Fair Play*, a sloop built at Red Bank, was running on this route. This endeavor was followed by others. Operations reached their height in 1852, when the Red Bank Steamboat Company built three vessels, and the Middletown and Shrewsbury Transportation Company completed two. At the southern tip of the

County was another center of shipbuilding. The industry flourished on the Manasquan River until the Manasquan Inlet became too shallow for the passage of ships with a greater draft than a large sailboat. With the skilled workers available, however, small craft were still built there in considerable numbers. Later, Brielle became a center for the construction of small boats. A variety of factors brought about the decline of ship-building as a major industry in the last quarter of the nineteenth century. The advent of the railroad meant a drop in the coastwise trade and a consequent decline in the demand for coastal vessels. And the timber supply was virtually then exhausted, as is shown in this 1882 account of the Township of Washington, on the shore side of Burlington County: "Within the past few years the heavy timber has been hewn down and utilized for ship-building until at present nothing but the shoots of scrub oaks, with a limited amount of pine timber, remain to mark the once rich forest."

### SALVAGE AND LIFESAVING

Of great consequence to shore people were shipwrecks. One Seaville (Cape May County) resident in recalling the 1840's, wrote:

In those days, the first look in the morning was toward the ocean with a spyglass for a possible wreck. The first I recall was the "Eudora" after which several girl babies of the region were named in 1849 and 1850. . . . Another vessel was loaded with huge heads of brown sugar from Barbados and an open hog's head was an irresistible temptation to school children to get stuck up.

Since shoals and other danger spots were not adequately marked, ships frequently ran aground on the Jersey shore. The wrecks occurred mainly in the fall and winter months, and their number lessened in the second half of the century as lighthouses and lifesaving stations were constructed.

Certain unscrupulous individuals took advantage of the wrecked ships, particularly in the earlier years.

Salvagers, or "wreckers" as they were called, kept within the pale of their calling usually and contented themselves with goods which floated ashore or were taken from a vessel which had been abandoned by captain and crew. There were instances, however, in which the wreckers lost a sense of honor even among themselves. In the winter of 1830 a ship from Liverpool, laden with dry-goods and hardware, was wrecked on Absecon Beach. The shore people "scented the prey" and many thronged over to the beach, eager for spoils. Soon neighbor was robbing neighbor; boxes were buried in the sand dunes, and once the hider had gone in quest of more plunder, another wrecker would dig them out and secrete them somewhere else. The night was bitterly cold and two men died in the undertakings.

Occasionally charges were made that ruses were employed to bring vessels ashore. It was claimed that false lights were used to lure the mariner on to the unfamiliar shore. On Long Beach Island, some said, it was once a custom to fasten a lantern to a mule's neck and then lead the animal along the beach on a dark night, hoping a ship's captain would mistake the light for that of another ship sailing farther inshore, a mistake which might result in a wrecked ship. Little proof was found for these tales, but public indignation became highly aroused in 1834 when a schooner was cast ashore near Barnegat Inlet and its merchandise stolen. The thieves were caught and convicted, but in spite of the suspicions of many, no charge was made of decoying vessels ashore.

In 1846 a committee from the New Jersey Legislature investigated the situation when, after a wreck on February 15, certain persons on shore were accused of refusing to render assistance to passengers and seamen and even of plundering the bodies of those drowned in the catastrophe; but the charges were not substantiated. It was found that the castaways were given help and that there was no wholesale plundering, although there was some pilferage. There was no proof that false lights had been used as a decoy.

It was evident, however, that some kind of responsible rescue service subsidized by the government should be established. The first aid to come from Congress was the establishment of a series of lighthouses. In 1823, one was built at Cape May by Federal authority. This was the second on the Jersey shore; the first, on Sandy Hook, had been built in 1761 by New York merchants, and was acquired later by the Federal Government. In 1828 Congress constructed Highland Light on the Navesink Highlands. In 1834 Barnegat Light was erected on the north end of Long Beach Island, and in 1839 Five Fathom Lightship was set up in Delaware Bay, 17 miles from Cape May Lighthouse. In 1848 came the construction of the first Little Egg Harbor Light, near the south end of Long Beach. In 1857 Absecon Lighthouse was established at the northeast end of Atlantic City. Later, the light at Hereford Inlet north of Wildwood was built, in 1874, and, in 1885, the one on Ludlam's Beach near Sea Isle City. By 1900 the Federal Government was maintaining 15 lighthouses and small beacons between Sandy Hook and Cape May.

The need to aid crews and passengers on vessels that had foundered was met to some extent by the development of lifesaving stations. As early as the second decade of the century, volunteer lifesaving crews were scattered along the shore. Most of them were composed of small bands of local fishermen. The assumption of Federal responsibility is ascribed to the efforts of William Newell, who later became Governor of New Jersey. Elected to Congress as a representative in 1848, he had long been eager to have the Federal Government sponsor more lifesaving services. In August of that year he succeeded in getting Congress to appropriate ten thousand dollars to provide surfboats and rockets for the protection of life and property on the New Jersey coast from Sandy Hook to Little Egg Harbor. This was the first appropriation from the Federal Government to any of the states for such work. Eight lifeboat houses were constructed. The following year, another appropriation was made for six stations between Little Egg Harbor and Cape May.

William Newell's work on the behalf of lifesaving continued. In 1850 the Scottish brig *Ayrshire*, with 201 English and Irish immigrants aboard, was wrecked on Absecon Beach. The rescue efforts employed an improvement on the breeches buoy, developed by Newell. His special apparatus was used by a volunteer crew of fishermen. A yoke of oxen was brought to the shore. A ball fired from a mortar took a line out to the stranded vessel. Then a closed life-car, built by Joseph Francis of Toms River, was carried by its rings on the hawser, and in three minutes the first carload was safely drawn ashore over the roaring surf. The operation was repeated as frequently as heavy seas permitted, and within two days all except one person had been safely landed.

More widespread lifesaving facilities were provided in the second half of the century. By 1872, stations had been established on the average of every five miles along the shore, and in 1886 the Federal Government inaugurated the policy of manning all stations with paid crews. By 1900 there were 42 stations on the coast at an average of three miles apart. In the 20th century the lighthouses and the lifesaving stations became a part of the Coast Guard service.

By mid-nineteenth-century the era of the opening up of the shore through stagecoach routes and waterways was drawing to a close. These methods of transportation reached their height in the three decades before 1850. With the development of a railroad network, patronage decreased on both stagecoach lines and river boats, which slowly but steadily were discontinued. These changes were gradual and there was considerable overlapping, but the iron horse was an easy victor.

The coming of the railroad presaged a new era, and though it terminated a number of trades, it provided a stimulus to many others. It brought new life to the shore region and inaugurated a period of tremendous development for the shore resorts.

# PART II

# THE AGE OF THE IRON HORSE
## 1850–1900

# IV

## THE RAILROAD AND
## RESORT EXPANSION

---

There never has been a time when the resorts on
the New Jersey coast were so easy of access. . . .
From Philadelphia 9 express trains leave every
week, 2 additional on Saturday and 4 on Sunday.
. . . Such facilities place a trip to the seaside within
the reach of every class of persons.

*Woodbury Constitution,* August 13, 1884

The spread of the railroad network brought the democratization of the shore recreation industry. People could
now reach the vacation spots with a minimum of expense, in contrast to the costlier and more time consum-
ing trip by stage or steamboat. A Rutgers professor,
vacationing at Somers Point, noted in his journal for
July 20, 1867: "Before the railroad was built it took
two days for the trip to Philadephia. Now it is made in
one day, from two to three hours being taken for the
passage." Similarly, Walt Whitman observed in 1878
in a letter describing a railroad journey from Camden
to Atlantic City, "The whole route . . . has been literally
made and opened up to growth by the railroad." No
other single influence, except the evolution of the gasoline engine and thus the automobile and the truck,
proved so catalytic an agent in the development of the
shore.

In the interior of the State the railroad age began
earlier. The first track laid in New Jersey was at Bordentown in 1831. By 1833 the line was finished north to

South Amboy on the Raritan, and in January, 1834, south to Camden. The first railroad to the Jersey seashore was not built until 1854, when a line from Camden reached Absecon. By 1855, a bridge, carrying the road to the sea island which became Atlantic City, was finished, and so the first railroad to the seashore was opened. Although Cape May devotees urged the building of a line to their city, the resort did not achieve rail connections until nearly a decade later. Pessimists claimed that the route from Camden to Cape Island lay over unsatisfactory upland grades and that, anyway, Absecon Island was more readily accessible. Long Beach in Ocean County was about the same distance from Philadelphia as Absecon Beach, but the direct route from Camden to Long Beach cut through a much less productive pine area than the line already constructed. Furthermore, the Long Beach route involved the construction of a comparatively long causeway over Barnegat Bay at Manahawkin, while Absecon Island was closer to the mainland. No great demand existed at this time for seaside resorts in Monmouth County to attract New York City dwellers, who had sea beaches on nearby Long Island, while Philadephia's thousands had no ocean beach nearer than the Jersey shore.

While the line from Camden to Absecon was being built, skeptics belittled the effort. One group of people told the entrepreneurs, "a railroad with but one end" (that is, Camden) should never be built." Others said: "Build your road, and the people will starve to death when they get to the beach." Still others warned that the mosquitoes would drive summer visitors away. Absecon Island itself was called at that time "a succession of barren sand hills and unproductive swamps."

The Camden and Atlantic Railroad cost about one million eight hundred thousand dollars to construct, which was more than the original estimate of its cost. The gross receipts in 1854 were one hundred seventeen thousand dollars but in the Panic of 1857 the road went into bankruptcy. It was reorganized and the debt reduced. By the 1860's traffic had greatly increased, the road became prosperous, and the gross receipts rose to five hundred sixty-four thousand dollars in 1876. Soon other investors sought to participate in so profitable a flow of traffic, and in 1877 the Philadelphia and Atlantic Railroad was completed to Atlantic City, by way of Pleasantville, in the record time of 90 days. The roadbed for the "Narrow Gauge" line was easier to build than that of the Camden and Atlantic, for it had a three-and-a-half-foot gauge instead of the standard four feet, eight and a half inches. Later, after the Reading Railroad bought it, the gauge was made standard. The third and last railroad to reach Atlantic City was built in 1880 by the Pennsylvania Railroad from Newfield, as a branch from its West Jersey Cape May line.

Other lines were constructed in three years to reach other resorts of the central shore. A road was pushed to Brigantine Beach north of Atlantic City. This joined the Narrow Gauge at Brigantine Junction, just below Cologne. In 1880, a short line, eight miles long, was completed between Pleasantville, on the Narrow Gauge, to Somers Point, serving the communities of Bakersville and Smiths Landing. The primary purpose of this narrow-gauge line was to provide access to the new resort of Ocean City. It was claimed that with this line and the steamboat it now took only a little longer to get to Ocean City than to Atlantic City. Roundtrip tickets good for ten days were sold, Philadelphia to Ocean City, for $1.65.

Two railroad lines were eventually built to Cape May. The first one was completed, despite the exigencies of war, on August 22, 1863. Known as the Cape May and Millville Railroad, it joined at Millville with the Glassboro and Millville Railroad. To attract visitors this railroad company built the "Excursion House" at Cape May in 1868. According to a contemporary account, it was "the most convenient building perhaps in the world." The trains ran direct to the House, "dispensing with that vexatious hunt for quarters so annoying to excursionists."

The second railroad did not reach Cape May until nearly three decades later, although the need for competitive railroad service had been recognized for several years. It was finally completed in 1894 by the Reading Railroad. The resort declared a holiday to celebrate, with city officials, civic organizations, and the fire department surrounding the new station where a large welcome arch had been erected. Lack of the anticipated traffic, however, caused a receiver to be appointed for the road in August of the same year.

Favored with accessibility by sea, the Monmouth County shore waited longer for the iron horse. A dozen years after Atlantic City got her railroad, in 1867, the Farmingdale and Squan Village Railroad Company constructed a road to Squan Village, now Manasquan, and a line was thus completed from Jamesburg, on the Camden and Amboy, to the seacoast. The road, however, that best served the region for the New York trade was the New York and Long Branch Railroad, chartered in 1869, but not built until the mid-seventies. This joined the main line of the New Jersey Central Railroad at Elizabethport, and gave Long Branch direct rail service up to the ferry across the Hudson.

Another line, incorporated in 1863, was built to serve the immediate seashore. Called the Long Branch and Sea-Shore Railroad, it was planned to follow a route from a point on Sandy Hook south to Long Branch. Later the terminus of the road was moved to Spermaceti Cove at the base of Sandy Hook, from which a line of steamers ran to New York. In 1865 the road was extended down the sea island to Long Branch, "so close to the ocean beach in some places that the surf blends with the rattle of the cars and the shriek of the locomotive whistle; and at times in high tides, the waves have washed over the track." A few years later, when the New York and Long Branch Railroad was completed, much of the traffic was diverted to the all-rail route from Long

Branch to Jersey City. In 1876 railroad connections were completed south of Long Branch as far as Sea Girt and Manasquan Village. "This road," declared a contemporary account, "promises to bring about a wonderful change in the future." Later the Manasquan was bridged and connections made at Bay Head and Point Pleasant.

The first real rail facility to the Ocean County Shore came in 1866 when a spur from Manchester (Lakehurst) on the Delaware and Raritan Line was built to Toms River. By 1871 this branch line had pushed south to Forked River and Waretown. In 1871 another spur was built to Tuckerton from Whiting by businessmen from Tuckerton and Philadelphia who were interested in the summer resort possibilities at Beach Haven. In 1872 the owners built a short line down to Little Egg Harbor Bay, and a steamboat was placed in commission between Long Beach Island and the mainland. In the middle 1880's the Manahawkin and Long Beach Transportation Company, which was later absorbed by the Pennsylvania when it took over the Tuckerton line, built a spur on a trestle across Manahawkin Bay to Long Beach, and a line was constructed south to Beach Haven and north to Harvey Cedars and Barnegat City on the Inlet.

The Ocean County Island Beach resorts were served in 1883 when the Pennsylvania, aiming at the sea resort trade, leased the Camden-Pemberton road and extended it through the pine barrens to the south bank of the Toms River. From there it crossed upper Barnegat Bay on a trestle over to the southern end of Island Beach to what became Seaside Park. From Seaside Park the line was pushed north along Island Beach through what became Lavallette, Chadwick, and Mantoloking to meet the Long Branch Railroad which had been built south to Point Pleasant and Bay Head.

Railroad travel to the shore in these early days was far from comfortable. The first train between Camden and Atlantic City did not provide de luxe transportation. One conductor recalled that the engine was a smoky woodburner, which caused the passengers considerable annoyance. There were no signals of any kind. The cars held 40 persons each. The seats were plain boards, not even cushioned. Most of the cars were open coaches. "My!" declared the conductor, "how the dust did fly!"

The conductors in those days did not punch tickets. Persons who got aboard at Camden had tickets, but those who got on at various stations paid their fares to the conductor in cash. On the return to Camden the receipts were turned in. The conductor's salary was thirty dollars a month, but extra income was procured from express charges on packages. For this the conductors charged what the traffic would bear; the minimum fee was twenty-five cents. They carried parcels and letters, and provided, after a fashion, banking services. One conductor said he carried thousands of dollars from different places and received a dollar for every one thousand dollar transaction. Later the Pennsylvania Railroad secured control; salaries were increased to sixty dollars a month and all perquisites were forbidden. At this time a new system of selling and canceling tickets became effective.

The impact of the new railroads on the shore economy was striking. Until the 1850's, most of the area had remained comparatively undeveloped. The coast villages, isolated from nearby cities, continued largely dependent upon the sea. With the transportation facilities offered by the new railroads, however, the shore became easily accessible to the mounting population of the Newark-New York metropolitan area as well as that of the Camden-Philadelphia region, and a huge expansion of the seaside population ensued. In 1850, the last Census before the coming of the railroad, the population of the four coastal counties was fifty-five thousand seven hundred. By 1885, it had risen to one hundred eleven thousand, doubling in 35 years. Before the railroad came to Absecon Island, the site of present-day Atlantic City and its suburbs of Ventnor, Margate, and Longport, less than half a dozen families lived there. The railroads made Atlantic City New Jersey's premier resort. It reported a population of seven hundred in 1860. By 1900,

# STAGECOACH

In 1865, New Yorkers still came to the northern Jersey shore via steamboat and stagecoach. Here their objective is Squan and on to Point Pleasant boarding houses.

**UNITED STATES MAIL**

FOR

**SQUAN VILLAGE,**

VIA

**EATON TOWN, SHARK RIVER, AND NEW BEDFORD.**

Passengers for this Line will take the new and splendid Steamer OCEAN WAVE, from the foot of Jay Street, North River, EVERY DAY. For time of departure see Bills. Extra Stages will be in readiness to convey passengers to Point Pleasant Boarding Houses, and elsewhere.

**FARE.**

**From New-York to Squan Village, 87½c.**

**TICKETS TO BE HAD ON BOARD THE BOAT.**

**E. R. HAIGHT, Proprietor.**

**ALL BAGGAGE AT THE RISK OF THE OWNERS.**

June 30th, 1865.

Nesbitt & Co., Printers, New-York.

# BARNEGAT LIGHT

The Barnegat lighthouse is on the tip of Long Beach Island, south of Barnegat Inlet. Built in 1834, it had to be rebuilt in 1858 because of beach erosion, and now reaches a height of 165 feet.

## "BIG SEA DAY"

Farmers of southern Monmouth County drove their families to Manasquan for their annually observed "Big Sea Day," which was in a way a continuation of an Indian custom from long ago. The blankets on the buggies provided bathhouse facilities in 1896.

*Courtesy J. Stanley DuBois, Manasquan*

## COLEMAN HOUSE

This picture of the Coleman House in Asbury Park, taken in 1876, shows a typical form of vehicular transportation. Note also the cluster of lady vacationers on the commodious porch and the Mansard roof topping the structure.

*Courtesy Asbury Park Press*

## GERMANTOWN COTTAGE

This was the elaborate summer house in Atlantic City of a German-town family. The time is 1878; here is the "gingerbread" of the period.

*From Atlas of the New Jersey Coast, 1878*

These are bathing costumes worn at Atlantic City about 1875.

*Courtesy Free Public Library, Trenton*

# AN EARLY BOARDWALK

The first boardwalks were made in sections for easy removal in time
of storm and for winter storage.

## OCEAN GROVE, 1878

The boardwalk is laid directly on the beach, as the first "boardwalks"
were just that. At left is a boat used by the beach's lifeguards.

## CAPE MAY, 1878

In the foreground are elegant equipages from horse-drawn omnibus to barouche. In the background is Chalfonte House.

*From Atlas of the New Jersey Coast, 1878*

## SUMMER CAPITAL

This house was given to President Grant by a group of wealthy Elberon summer residents. The President shared their preference for this part of the Jersey shore and spent several seasons here.

*Courtesy Asbury Park Press*

# IRON PIER

The Iron Pier was built at Long Branch in 1878. It extended six hundred feet out into the ocean. A heavy storm in 1881 washed it away.

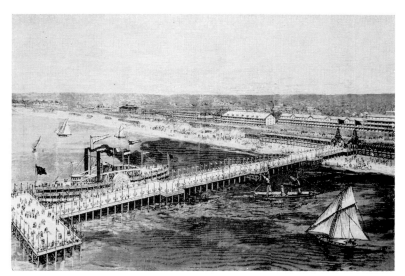

# A 1907 AUTO

This picture was taken at the corner of Main and Water Streets in Toms River. Note the interest on the part of bystanders.

# STORM

The scene is Ocean City after the devastating storm of March, 1962.
Note, at left center, two cottages burning at edge of beach.

*Courtesy Philadelphia Evening Bulletin*

it had grown to twenty-eight thousand. The rate of population increase for this resort between 1870 and 1880 was 425 per cent and from 1890 to 1900, 113 per cent.

The coming of the railroad did not put an end to the horse and buggy; the horse still served all localities for local transportation, and continued to be a major influence in the lives of all shore people until the development of the automobile. However, the railroad did end the age of the stagecoach and the freight wagon, but the change-over was gradual. Similarly, the influence of the railroad on shore life diminished slowly. The competition of the automobile was not evident until the 1920's.

A book published in 1868 included considerable commentary on the impact of the first railroads on the growth of Atlantic City. The author hoped that the "iron horse . . . with his snort of enterprise and puff of power may long live to lend the music and enchantment of advancing civilization to the wilds of New Jersey." The expansion of resorts along the Jersey seashore became abiding testimonials to this "snort of enterprise and puff of power." The area passed through its period of greatest growth between 1850 and 1900. After 1900 new growth was mainly in the form of increasing populations and not in the foundation of new resorts.

The Monmouth County seashore had special attractions for vacationers. Much of the Monmouth shoreline was on the mainland, while most of the resorts in the other three counties were on the sea islands. North of Long Branch the mainland was fronted by a sea island, but south of that resort it lay directly on the ocean. Monmouth's thirty miles of coastline embraced locations from Sandy Hook south to Manasquan and Brielle, most of which were developed between 1850 and 1900. South of Sandy Hook, which was Federal property from 1790, was Sea Bright, purchased in 1865 by a Freehold physician at five dollars an acre. By the late 1880's some lots were selling at the rate of seven thousand dollars an acre. Stages ran to Sea Bright from the station at Oceanic, for twenty-five cents a trip. Development at nearby Monmouth Beach began in 1871, and by 1889 so many summer residences had been erected that there was scarcely a stretch of two hundred yards without a cottage.

Long Branch maintained its preëminence among the County's resorts throughout most of this period. By the 1870's it was the best known of the New Jersey resorts, thanks to the New York and Long Branch Railroad. The resort aimed at exclusiveness and endeavored to attract wealthy people. It began to decline as a fashionable resort, however, during the 1880's. New developments outside its boundaries attracted some of its clientele. The constant erosion of the five-mile bluff along the ocean, which had been the resort's special pride, led promoters to avoid the area. At this time the bluff was estimated to be wearing away at a rate of four feet every ten years, but the rate was increased by the battering of severe winter storms. A seawall was recommended to save the buildings but hotelkeepers argued that it would destroy the bathing beach at the foot of the bluff, and the plan was abandoned. Many residents were forced to move their houses back from the sea.

The permanent population of Long Branch grew steadily during this whole period and did not reflect the drop in summer residents. It became a city in 1867. In the 1880 Census it numbered 3,833 inhabitants, and in the next ten years it nearly doubled its population, with a return in the 1890 Census of 7,231. In 1900 it reported 8,872 residents. By this time, Asbury Park had begun to threaten its supremacy as a resort. Its emergence as a city of some industrial consequence did not occur until the twentieth century.

Two other resorts near Long Branch developed toward the end of the century, Elberon and Deal. The land on which Elberon was built was purchased by promoter Lewis B. Brown in the 1870's, and the place gradually became an exclusive resort. Deal was mentioned in the 1834 *Gazetteer* as having several boarding houses. In the late 1890's real estate promoters began to buy property there, and in 1898 it was incorporated as a borough.

Nearby Deal Lake was an attraction. Once an ocean inlet, it was turned into a fresh water lake when James A. Bradley, founder of Asbury Park, had a three-mile-long dike constructed.

Ocean Grove was founded by the Methodist Camp-Meeting Association in 1869. Its history was closely intertwined with that of Asbury Park which became the largest of the Monmouth County resorts. In 1870 the first lots at Ocean Grove were leased at auction; the highest price paid was seventy-five dollars. By 1885 lots that had been bought along the ocean front were leased for as much as one thousand five hundred dollars. The lots were not deeded outright, but rented by the Camp-Meeting Association to prevent "anyone offensive next to your cottage." Tents with a floor and a small kitchen in the rear could be rented from the Association for two and a half dollars per week, for not less than two weeks. The rental had to be paid in advance. By 1871 two hundred tents on permanent floors were in use, and by 1879 this had increased to seven hundred. The Grove was referred to as a "little canvas village" at that time. By 1874 over two hundred Methodist ministers were present during the annual Camp Meeting and many of them participated in the services.

In 1870 Ocean Grove was six miles from the nearest railroad station, at Long Branch, which was reached by stage. Direct railroad connections were desired, and in 1872 the Association subscribed ten thousand dollars toward financing one, but it was not until 1875 that the first train arrived at the Asbury Park–Ocean Grove station from New York. Shortly afterward, the track was completed south to Manasquan, where connections were made to Philadelphia. In 1873 it was estimated that twenty-five thousand people had come to Ocean Grove by one route or the other.

In 1870 five hundred acres north of Wesley Lake, on the south side of which lay Ocean Grove, came upon the market. Members of the Ocean Grove Camp-Meeting Association feared that the tract might fall into the hands of people not in sympathy with the mode of living at the Grove. The land was bought in the fall of that year by James Bradley, who named it after Bishop Asbury of the Methodist Church.

Asbury Park grew rapidly. According to a guidebook published in 1889, the Park had a permanent population of more than three thousand, and over thirty thousand visitors in the summer. There were nearly two hundred hotels and boarding houses and about eight hundred private residences. The assessed valuation, which had been sixteen thousand dollars in 1870, was almost two million dollars in 1889.

More resorts were established in the eighteen nineties in the southern part of the county. These included Bradley Beach, Avon-by-the-Sea (originally known as Key East), Belmar, Como, and Spring Lake. Sea Girt was promoted by Commodore Stockton of Princeton. Having recently returned from his adventures in the Mexican War as a hero, he bought the land in 1852 for fifteen thousand dollars. The Commodore built Stockton Mansion, which later became a part of the Beach House. In 1875 a railroad from Farmingdale and Freehold was extended to Sea Girt, but it was better served by the railroad that pushed south down the coast through Asbury Park in the same year, which gave it speedy connection with New York. In 1884 the State bought land in Sea Girt for a National Guard camp, and the site was enlarged by further purchases in 1887. Rifle ranges were erected at the ocean extremity of the State grounds.

Squan was founded in 1825 on the Manasquan River inlet, but not as a resort. In 1845, 27 boat departures were reported from the inlet, mostly for New York with cargoes of wood and charcoal. A wheelwright shop was later located there and some of the first heavy wagons used by the lifesaving stations were built. "Manasquan is . . . more a farming town than a summer resort," noted a guidebook of 1889. Eventually summer cottages were erected on the beach and at the mouth of the inlet.

Nearby on Manasquan River was Brielle, which later became a center for building small craft. The Brielle Land Association, incorporated in 1881, purchased a tract of a hundred and fifty acres there for lots, and a hotel was built in the later 1880's. Many cottages were constructed, and the Association ran a free stage for the hotel guests and cottagers to the ocean beach at Manasquan.

During the same period Ocean County experienced a growth in resorts similar to that in Monmouth County. Most of the locations already established by 1850 continued to develop, although Tucker's Beach declined. Point Pleasant became a borough in 1866. The cause of its growth was the extension into the area of the two railroads noted above. By 1899 it was a flourishing summer town with trolleys, electric lights, a newspaper, five churches, four hotels and another under construction. At the head of Barnegat Bay, Bay Head, the terminus of the New York and Long Branch Railroad, was incorporated as a borough in 1886. Projecting southward from Bay Head to Barnegat Inlet, a distance of twenty miles, was a peninsula called Island Beach, on which a series of resorts grew up between 1850 and 1900, especially after the railroad's arrival in 1883. These included Seaside Park, organized as a borough in 1898, and Lavallette, which became a separate entity in 1887. Chadwicks, farther north, Mantoloking, and Seaside Heights were developments of the twentieth century.

Long Beach, the resort "six miles at sea," was the second Ocean County area to expand as a summer vacation center. The central and northern ends of the island developed in the last half of the century, especially after the railroad crossed Barnegat Bay at Manahawkin in the 1880's eliminating the ferry ride. In 1881 Barnegat City was founded at the northern tip on Barnegat Inlet. The next year the Peahala Club was organized and gave its name to a community. Beach Haven was detached from a mainland township and organized as a borough in 1890. Harvey Cedars, once the site of a whale fishery, separated itself from a mainland township in 1894. One of the chief reasons for this withdrawal from the mainland townships was to provide funds for the development of the seaside area itself through local taxation.

Wide development in these years occurred in Atlantic County resorts. Absecon Island remained unchanged until 1855. With the advent of the railroad, Atlantic City flourished mightily. By 1859 it had 130 buildings, including boarding houses, three churches, a schoolhouse, a market, and a lighthouse. The decade of the highest percentage of growth occurred in the 1870's when its permanent population more than quadrupled. Cheaper transportation rates followed the building of the Narrow Gauge railroad.

The residents of Philadelphia were sometimes bombarded with brochures on the advantages of coming to Atlantic City. In 1873, the Camden and Atlantic Railroad published a pamphlet, "To the Sea-Shore," in which Philadelphians were advised:

. . . housetops and pavements reflect back the heat. . . . Nature is parched and lifeless and from down the street comes the cloud of dust. . . . Man, woman, and beast are all in sweltering discomfort. The invalid, pale and wan, seeks some shady nook and fans away the weary day, dreaming the while of some sequestered spot down by the sea. . . . So step, in a moment, from the suffocation of bricks and mortar to the stimulating breath of old ocean. There are six trains daily with two extras on Sunday.

As early as 1857 a hotel had been built at Brigantine Beach north of Atlantic City across the inlet. In 1892 a land development company sold many lots on the island and helped sponsor the construction of a railroad in 1897. That same year Brigantine separated itself from the mainland township of Galloway. Its development, however, was adversely affected by the destruction of the railroad trestle in a severe September storm in 1903. The railroad company was unable to rebuild the connection, and it was not until 1924 that a bridge to

Atlantic City was constructed, after which Brigantine experienced again a brief land boom.

South of Atlantic City is Margate; it was called South Atlantic City when it was incorporated in 1897. Between it and Atlantic City is Ventnor, organized as a city in 1903. On the southern tip of Absecon Island is Longport, where acreage was purchased in 1882 for development. The first train entered Longport in 1884 from Atlantic City; and it was organized as a borough in 1898.

One reason Atlantic City did not extend further on the island was the existence of the "Dry Inlet." Absecon Island had been divided for many years by this shallow inlet through which the tide flowed and ebbed. When Atlantic City was chartered by the Legislature in 1854, its boundaries extended from Absecon Inlet southward to the "Dry Inlet." After the inlet gradually filled in, it became Jackson Avenue, but its effect as a barrier was more permanent.

The railroad stimulated wide growth in the sea islands of Cape May County between 1850 and 1900. As late as 1844 one commentator wrote of the County, "Along the seaside, several beaches known as Two-Mile Beach, Five-Mile Beach, . . . Seven-Mile Beach, Ludlam's Beach, and Peck's Beach extend the whole length of the County." They were covered with grass and afforded excellent pasturage. Here was centered the cattle industry, discussed above. In the last half of the nineteenth century Peck's Beach became Ocean City; Ludlam's Beach, Strathmere and Sea Isle City; Five-Mile Beach, Anglesea and the Wildwoods; Seven-Mile Beach became Avalon and Stone Harbor; and, in the period following 1900, Two-Mile Beach became Cold Spring Harbor.

It was not easy to reach Peck's Beach at first. A stage-coach line ran from Camden to Beesleys Point on Great Egg Harbor, and from there a sailboat was used to convey boarders the two miles to the beach. When the railroad from Millville to Cape May reached South Seaville in the early 1860's a few more visitors came annually. They left the train at South Seaville and drove twelve miles by stagecoach over a sandy road. By 1866 plans were afoot for the establishment of what is now Ocean City, and in 1879 it came into existence as a Methodist temperance summer resort. In 1884 the first railroad was built onto the island when the Pennsylvania, which extended already to Sea Isle City, crossed Corson's Inlet and was run north to the head of the beach. In 1897, as traffic increased, the Reading Railroad built a spur into the resort from Tuckahoe.

Ocean City grew rapidly. In 1881 a large auditorium was built to accommodate the people attending camp meetings. By 1882 over a hundred houses and a school had been built. In 1897, three years after it became a borough, it was incorporated as a city.

Ludlam's Beach, south of Ocean City, across Corson's Inlet, had a six-and-a-half-mile frontage on the Atlantic. As late as 1850 there were no permanent residents. The area was purchased in 1880 by Charles K. Landis, who had already established Vineland, and Sea Isle City was built there. The first railroad connection was constructed in 1884, controlled by the Pennsylvania Railroad, and further facilities were provided in 1893 by the Reading Railroad. Sea Isle City, originally part of Dennis Township, became a borough in 1890. By 1900 it was reported to have thirty hotels and three hundred cottages.

Seven-Mile Beach, across Townsends Inlet from Sea Isle City, had been called Tatham's Beach while Henry Tatham of Philadelphia owned it and his "farm-house" was the only house in the area. Once Tatham sold the beach, it was necessary to get rid of the cattle, and gunmen were hired to shoot them. Avalon was founded in 1887 on the north end of Seven-Mile Beach by a group of Philadelphia promoters; by 1897, it was separated from Middle Township on the mainland. Stone Harbor, on the south end of the Beach, did not become a borough until after 1910. Access by wagon road was available from Swainton for Avalon and from Cape May Court House for Stone Harbor.

Five-Mile Beach, across Hereford Inlet, is the site of present-day Wildwood and North Wildwood. While still called Anglesea, North Wildwood was known as a fishing resort. It was reached by rail in 1885 and subsequently became a borough. In 1880 a realty company purchased land south of Anglesea for a resort named Holly Beach. The railroad pushed down from Anglesea, and it became a borough in 1885. Wildwood was founded next to Holly Beach by promoter Philip Baker of Vineland in 1890, on a tract of about a hundred acres, of which half was heavily wooded with some trees reaching a hundred feet. Wildwood, once part of Middle Township on the mainland, became a borough in 1897, and in 1912 Holly Beach and Wildwood merged.

The beginnings of Cape May have already been recounted. By 1848 it was large enough to separate itself from Lower Township. Two railroads built to serve it during this period occasioned further development. In 1875 a community two miles east of Cape May was established on the extreme land end of the Jersey shore. Surrounded on all sides except the northeast by water, it was originally called "Sea Grove" by its Philadelphia promoters, but its name changed to Cape May Point in 1878. It was here that John Wanamaker of Philadelphia had his summer home, and President Benjamin Harrison was given a summer cottage.

All the newly-established resorts suffered "'growing pains" as varied problems arose to face the visitors who sought to enjoy Victorian vacations at the shore.

# V

## VICTORIAN VACATIONS

---

> A broad-brimmed hat for the ladies is indispensable. . . . Simple medicines should also be taken to the seashore, especially for diarrhoea and constipation. . . . When people are going to stay in an elevated story of a hotel, a half inch rope as a fire escape may be a prudent provision . . . carry a small cord to be borne when bathing and thrown out for relief in peril.
>
> "Life at the Sea Shore,"
> published at Princeton, 1880

Visitors to the burgeoning resorts were submerged in advice. They were told what accoutrements to bring to the shore with them; they were given explicit admonitions concerning the right way to take a "sea-bath"; they were offered a variety of diversions. Life at Atlantic City centered along the newly constructed Boardwalk; Cape May and Long Branch glittered with fashionable and worldly amusements; while in some resorts, such as Ocean City and particularly Ocean Grove, rigorous restrictions reflected the influence of the church denomination that sponsored them.

Sea bathing was the outstanding attraction of all the resorts. "The surf lubricates the joints like oil," exclaimed one devotee of the sea bath in 1874, writing from Ocean Grove, the Methodist resort:

The long waves gently shock the frame and stir the sluggish blood into fresher motion. . . . The torpid liver finds itself compelled to join the general activity. . . . The rapid action of all the parts, . . . clears the throat from its huskiness and the voice peals out in laughter. . . . Grave men fling out their limbs like colts in pasture; dignified women . . . sport like girls at recess. . . . Young men and maidens forget how far society keeps them apart and together dash in, in entire forgetfulness of all society may think.

Detailed directions for the vacationers' bathing appeared in 1885 in a booklet, "Summer Days in New Jersey." Particularly illuminating was the section, "Rules for Bathing," which warned the visitor, "If your teeth are of the kind which did not grow in your mouth beware lest a wave knock them out." Before going into the surf the guests were told to "run briskly up and down the beach for ten minutes." If the ladies wore "any lacings around the chest," they were advised to "throw them off" and "let the lungs have a hearty chance for all the air they can take." If, by chance, "any cheerful or muscular fellow" was willing to race, the unattached damsel was advised to "have a foot-race right on the sand."

Once the preliminary "warming up" was finished, the vacationer was given instructions more suitable for a contortionist than a carefree sea-sojourner. "Now," he was told, "bounce through the surf with a hop, skip, and jump; hold your fingers to your ears and your thumbs to your nostrils, and put your head under the water. Now dance, leap, tumble, swim, kick, float, or make any other motions that seem good to you."

Today's reader might ponder whether he could hold his fingers to his ears and his thumbs to his nostrils and his head under the water. In such a stance it is questionable whether he could "dance, leap, tumble, swim, kick, float, or make any other motions that seem good."

Accommodations available for changing one's attire were, in the earlier years, non-existent. As it was described in an Ocean Grove pamphlet, the men at first went off to a distance, left their clothes on the beach, and took a dip in the "garb of nature." The women found another secluded spot where they enjoyed the surf in garments whose days of usefulness had passed. Later, as bathhouses were erected along the beach, more care had to be taken in bathing dress.

The boarding houses and hotels, which had been constructed at some distance from the water, found it necessary to line the beachfront with temporary accommodations for the visitors. At Atlantic City in the 1860's most guests walked to the beach from the hotels and boarding houses on Atlantic Avenue, although two hotels provided horse-car transportation to the bathhouses on the beach. These buildings were rough, unsightly structures so constructed that they could be put on a wagon every autumn and hauled away from the high winter waves. Long rows of bathhouses dumped along Pacific and other Avenues were a common winter sight; not a building was left on the beach after the close of the season. A few weeks before the summer season opened, the beachfront presented an animated picture as busy laborers restored the bathhouses and removed accumulated sand drifts and debris from winter wrecks. By the 1880's permanent and fairly substantial bathhouses had been built. These were provided with bulwarks, and the foundations were sunk deep into the sand.

Bathhouses at Cape May were described as places of "much confusion." In 1854, a young lady correspondent to a Washington, D.C., paper wrote her impressions of her first visit to "Cape Island." She gave a vivid and critical description of the women's bathhouse serving a well-known hotel. Apparently she was a bit overwhelmed by conditions.

Beside a large tub of water in the centre of the floor knelt or sat several ladies just from the surf in all the various stages of disrobing, each intent upon her own arrangement and utterly regardless of what was passing around her. Others were preparing for the bath, laying aside their dresses . . . while the latest comers were removing their shawls and bonnets and exchanging greetings with acquaintances. For the first few moments we were deafened and bewildered. The sight of some dozen females only partially dressed and in garments perfectly saturated with sea water . . . and parties of romping children apparently quite indifferent to the dense atmosphere . . . made us struggle for breath. Following the example of others, we changed our double wrapper for a woolen bathing suit, covered our hair and . . . on crossing the threshold were met by our male escort, equipped for the sea.

## LIFEGUARDS

No lifeguards were provided in the earlier years, and fear of drowning was always imminent. One Cape May visitor of 1845 tells of a "rescue rope" which she saw hanging on a bathhouse. This she considered inadequate. She noted two Newfoundland dogs among the bathers, which she thought might be trained for rescue work. She felt that what was most needed was the invention of some kind of "Life Preserver" to be used in moments of danger.

Volunteer lifeguards proved of some service, but the problem of recompense was a thorny one. The disadvantage of relying on the generosity of those who had been saved is shown in this story of one volunteer which appeared in a Salem newspaper in 1869: "Mr. Boynton, who has saved so many lives this season, . . . was offered 50¢ by one gentleman after he had been safely dragged ashore. Mr. Boynton handed him back 49¢ in change remarking that he did not usually accept more than a life was worth."

In 1865 13 people were drowned at Atlantic City. In 1868 a few of the hotel proprietors and bathhouse keepers put out fixed safety-lines so that the timid might have something to which to cling as they enjoyed the surf, but the venturesome still went beyond them and drownings continued to occur. It was not until 1872 that lifeguards were first hired. They were paid mainly from funds provided by the Camden and Atlantic Railroad Company, supplemented with donations from visitors. Many bathers were rescued that season, and more guards were hired during subsequent summers. The provision of guards became firmly established in the early 1880's when the City Council assumed responsibility for paying them. By the 1884 season, 25 were hired.

## BATHING COSTUMES

The question of what to wear when bathing often perplexed the shore visitors. In the earlier years, clothing for bathing was restricted to such cast-off garments as would most modestly meet the puritanical standards of the day. Although one commentator on shore etiquette declared as late as 1880: "If practicable as to weather and those present, they may go in naked. This latter may be the better way. But where there is a mixed company, or strangers," he warned, "a suit is necessary." For the most part the women wore twilled flannel coats fastened up to their necks, in brown, blue or gray. The tape-trimmed ruffles almost covered their hands. The coat, it was advised, must "fit loose" and it was recommended that it "be buttoned and not tied." Long full pantalettes clung closely around the ankles. A wide coarse straw hat tied under the chin in the shape of a poke completed the costume, for in those days sunburn was a disgrace. The men wore loose, flapping top garments similar to those of the women. In place of the pantalettes were loose trousers. Whether the head was bald or well-thatched, it was covered with a small skull cap or straw hat held in place by a string of turkey-red.

The whole matter of bathing customs distressed foreign visitors considerably. One Englishwoman maintained in 1876 that the situation was not on a par with similar conditions abroad. "Bathing customs . . . could hardly be worse," she complained in describing Long Branch. The rows of huts on the shore in front of each hotel, she said, were unpainted and "often even unplaned." They were nailed together with sides and roof of the same material and were "as incapable of keeping out wind and rain as so many paper boxes." The English-woman also spoke scornfully of piles of "damp and clammy" faded woolen garments which "they facetiously denominate 'bathing dresses' and which they let to ladies and gentlemen at the rate of one-half dollar for each bath." She declared tartly, "That so many Americans are to be found who are willing to put the suits on and walk unflinchingly across the stretch of sand between the disrobing hut and the surf under the fire of hundreds of glances . . . is proof that the bravery of the nation should not be lightly impugned."

In contrast to the American bathing dress, observed the same visitor, French ladies selected their bathing outfits with great care. One of the latter might wear "a delicate rose flannel, with pleatings of silk, with hat trimmed in accordance." With this the bather would wear pink hose and straw shoes. Another outfit might be of navy blue serge with stripes of yellow or some other tasteful combination. In New Jersey, the women's bathing dresses were almost always of a coarse, dark flannel, much too large, and crowned with a rough straw hat more fit for a gutter than a lady's head. "And as for the gentlemen!" the English observer shuddered. "What scarecrows they are! Description could do them no justice."

## ON THE BOARDWALK

One of the outstanding facilities for recreation at the larger shore resorts was the "boardwalk." Local writers waxed eloquent about its attractions. One Atlantic City native son rhapsodized in 1904: "It is an endless dress parade . . . in which everybody is one of the reviewers as well as one of the reviewed. The animation, the overflowing good nature, the laughter and contagious hilarity of the restless throng is irresistible. . . . Nowhere in the world is there such a kaleidoscope of beauty!"

The title for the promenade was adopted only after much discussion. The first one at Atlantic City, as elsewhere, was no more than a plank walk along the beach laid to keep people's feet out of the sand, and it was referred to simply as the "board walk." More elaborate walks were built later, but the name remained. In 1896, when a new and expensive promenade was dedicated there, people sought a more elegant title. Some suggested the use of the Italian "Rialto"; others, under English and French influence, urged that it be called the "Esplanade," but the original American appellation won when, in 1896, the City Council passed a resolution that the name "Boardwalk" be official.

Authorities disagree when and where the first boardwalk was built. Probably the early ones were so simple that people did not think them worth commenting on. Cape May adherents claim the first one was erected there. One spokesman for that resort noted that a boardwalk already constructed there was extended in 1868, and was then long enough to be dubbed "flirtation walk." The first walk at Ocean Grove consisted of a path two planks wide, laid lengthwise along stringers. This was widened in 1877 to a walk six feet wide, lighted by 21 lamps. In 1880 it was widened to 16 feet.

The first boardwalk of any great length was built at Atlantic City. In 1870, when the beach was described as a "wild public common with a scattering of bathhouses and areas of mosquito marsh and soft sand," a plan for one was presented to the City Council. Considerable opposition developed because, it was argued, such a walk would draw business from the main avenues two blocks back from the shore, and so it did later. Nevertheless, the proposal was finally accepted. The city, having no funds for building, found it necessary to issue script payable the following season. This script was accepted by the owner of the United States Hotel and by interested Philadelphia lumber merchants. A short time later, five thousand dollars in city bonds were sold at a discount of ten percent and with this money, which retired the script, the first boardwalk was built. The walk was eight feet wide. Most of it lay flat on the sand but some was set on pilings three feet above the beach. It extended from the lighthouse near the inlet to Missouri Avenue. During the winter season, when storm tides might wreck it, the walk was piled up in sections and secured. It was raised at street ends and under the elevation "saddle horses, work-horses, wagons, and other vehicles passed conveniently to the strand."

All boardwalks were vulnerable to storms. At Atlantic City in 1879, after storm damage, a new 16-foot walk was constructed. Damaged by severe storms during the winter of 1883–1884, it was rebuilt in the spring of 1884 in a more substantial manner. In 1890, after another storm almost completely demolished it, it was rebuilt on wooden piling, higher, wider, and stronger. This walk was the first to have railings. The first walks needed none, as they were so close to the sand, but the one built in 1884 was five feet high and only 20 feet wide. Many strollers fell off, some of whom suffered broken bones. A contemporary newspaper commented on the fallen: "Most of them were flirting. . . . They fell off when they turned around to get another smile or wink." The wooden railings on the latest walk, however, were not complete safeguards. One day 25 visitors fell into the sand "while leaning over the railing to watch beer garden waitresses and female performers bathe."

In 1896 the city fathers decided the promenade needed a steel underpinning, supported on wooden piling and special framework. All previous ones had been built entirely of wood. This time, the piling was sunk ten feet in the sand. The walk was widened to 40 feet in its main section and extended to a length of four miles. Further extensions were made in 1902, and a few years later the walk was joined to Ventnor's, which with Margate's provided a wooden walk eight miles long on the ocean front of Absecon Island. Concrete was applied to the steel frame to prevent rust and corrosion and finally, following the devastating hurricane of 1944, all the old wooden framework was replaced by steel and concrete.

Various recreation facilities soon abutted the boardwalk. The first amusement ride was a thriller later to be known as a Ferris Wheel. It was erected near the walk in 1871–1872. The "Epicycloidal Wheel" consisted of four huge wheels set at right angles to each other.

Each wheel revolved and each carried eight gondolas holding two people.

Piers built out into the ocean offered further spots for relaxation. Their number was limited by restrictions made at the time the City Council gained control over the beach. The Beach Park Act, passed by the Legislature in 1894, authorized the city to assume authority over the entire beach, and in 1896 easement deeds gave the city virtual ownership of most of it. These deeds allowed anyone owning property that fronted on the Boardwalk to erect a pier out into the ocean. It was specified, however, that any such pier must be at least a thousand feet in length, a restriction which effectively limited their number. Only four piers were built, not only because of the initial cost but also because of the probable lack of profit if too many were constructed, and the threat of destruction by storm was a constant deterrent.

The earlier piers were constructed before the thousand-foot qualification was put into effect. The first, erected in 1881, was destroyed by a storm tide in September, 1882. Rebuilt to a length of 865 feet, it was again wrecked in 1894. In 1883 the forerunner of what became Young's Ocean Pier was erected at the end of Tennessee Avenue, 850 feet in length. Wrecked in 1884, it was rebuilt and extended in 1898 by John Young. It then reached three thousand feet out into the ocean and was called "a delightful breathing place on a warm day." Advertised as "Young's Million Dollar Pier," it was so widely publicized that in 1906 a popular song, entitled "Roller Skating, Young's New Million Dollar Pier Song," was written about it. The chorus went:

> There, take my Kate,
> For a roller skate
> On Young's Million Dollar Pier.

A third pier was built in 1887 at the foot of Massachusetts Avenue and called the "Iron Pier." It was later sold to Heinz and Company of Pittsburgh for advertising purposes. In 1898 the famous Steel Pier Company built its first pier at the foot of Virginia Avenue, extending it 1,650 feet into the ocean.

## Taffy from the Sea

In the later nineteenth century the introduction of "salt water taffy," which was not made of salt water, started a new product which became a specialty. Visitors were delighted to have an opportunity to send a characteristic sweet to friends back home. According to one version, salt water taffy was first made in 1883 by David Bradley, whose small candy stand was on the seaside of the Boardwalk just two steps above sand level. There he specialized in taffy. One night, the local legend goes, a generous fullmoon tide brought a lively surf which dampened his stock. The next morning, after he had wiped off his sweets, a little girl stopped by and asked for some taffy. Mr Bradley queried, "You mean 'salt water taffy,' don't you?" The small customer seemed to like the candy, and Bradley's sister and mother, who had overheard the remark, later declared that to be a good name on which to capitalize. Bradley suggested making the taffy with ocean water, but his mother advocated changing only the name. The taffy was prepared by the regular recipe. When the 1884 season opened, Bradley ordered muslin signs lettered "Salt Water Taffy." Soon the business began to boom, and by the end of this period other concerns were offering a similarly named product. This gave rise to a local industry that by the 1940's shipped out over three million pounds of the taffy in one season.

Other forms of recreation more closely identified with the sea were available. In addition to fishing from the piers and the bridges across the inlets, crabbing was a favorite pastime. In a flowery explanation written in 1878, crabbing in the thoroughfare between Atlantic City and the mainland was called "a less venturesome sport, affording great delight to the ladies in particular. . . . While indulging in harmless sport, they are insensibly sipping the elixir of health from nature's laboratory."

At the more fashionable resorts, wholly different forms of diversions developed, including dancing and gambling, in great contrast to the religious activities at the new camp meeting locations.

# VI

## THE FASHIONABLE RESORTS
## AND CAMP MEETING LIFE

If our subscribers want a fast place, let them go
to Saratoga. . . . People who are content to dwell
in decencies should go to Cape May, while those
who like a spice of everything should patronize
Long Branch.

*New York Herald*, 1852

Cape May first held the title of the most fashionable
resort on the Jersey shore. The wealthy flocked there,
and Cape May reached the peak of its popularity in the
decade prior to the Civil War. By 1850 it was estimated
that a total of seventeen thousand visitors had been
entertained there that season. To its hotels and cottages
came rich Philadelphians, New Yorkers, and Baltimoreans and guests from many southern cities.

This was the era of the big hotels. In 1853 a typical
one, the Mount Vernon Hotel, locally called the largest
in the world, was opened, and its fame helped to pop-
ularize Cape May. The front section was three hundred
feet long and four stories high and one wing was five
hundred feet long and three stories high. It contained
482 rooms, with a bath in each room, an unusual feature
for that period. A guest in 1855 said that 750 patrons
were served in the dining room at one time and that it
took 250 steps to cross the floor.

Social life centered around the large hostelries. The
bigger houses vied with each other to offer the most attractions. Dancing was a main feature, and famous bands

were brought in by enterprising hosts. The events of the season were the grand balls which were usually held in the large dining hall, although some of the most fashionable establishments possessed separate ballrooms. One contemporary commentator describing Congress Hall in the 1850's, exclaimed:

Think of a hall 200 feet long, 45 feet wide, and 16 feet to the ceiling, without a pillar or post outside of its walls for a support! . . . At night, when this hall is cleared of its tables and chairs, and hundreds of gas jets are brilliantly burning and flickering, and the gay and élite are flushed with the giddy dance, then you behold a ball, . . . beautiful and fair.

The fame of Cape May was capitalized on by writers of popular songs. In 1855 one music company published the "Cape May Polka." In 1868 appeared "On the Beach at Cape May, a Schottische," and the following year brought with it "The Stockton House Quadrille." The most sentimental of those songs was written that same year, "In the Moonlight at Cape May," the chorus of which concluded:

> We spoke about the sweet moonlight
> While the moments passed away.
> We walked on, I was so happy
> In the moonlight at Cape May.

The wide hotel porches afforded opportunities for social gatherings and promenades. They were furnished with comfortable rockers and chairs and tables for cards and drinks. The bigger hotels boasted that their pianos were special kinds of instruments, "most of which came from Vienna and had that peculiar tone which they caught from the damp sea-air which rusted the wire and softened the dampers and made the music sound like the blowing of the northeast wind through a girl's wet hair."

The ladies wore gowns of the most extreme mode. When hoop skirts were being worn, they were the largest possible. One young matron found her costume a source of some embarrassment. While she was attending a

church service, her hoop skirt became hopelessly en-
tangled in the pew. The sexton and two gentlemen
struggled in vain to extricate her; finally the former said,
"Cant her [tip her], gentlemen, cant her." This was done
with success despite the protests of the lady, and much to
her consternation. Hoop skirts gave rise to the term
"teetering," which was applied to the goose gait affected
by fashionable young ladies.

In addition to the "sea-bathing," popular forms of
recreation at Cape May included gambling, drives in
beautifully appointed carriages, and last, but by no
means least, the opportunity to gaze at and talk about
famous visitors.

By 1840 there were already gambling clubs at the
resort. Wealthy Southern planters and nationally prominent visitors were devotees of the games of chance. The
most popular club was the "Blue Pig," at the ocean end
of Congress Hall's six-acre lawn. Here one dashing New
York widow was said to have won around fifty thousand
dollars in one evening. There were two other well-
patronized gambling clubs, one of which had a room
without windows or visible door. The noted Tennessee
gambler, Pettibone, spent several seasons at the Cape,
and his marital affairs created considerable interest. Mar-
ried three times, Pettibone caused some raising of eye-
brows when he re-married his first wife.

Wealthy Southerners and rich Northerners alike were
connoisseurs of horseflesh, and driving beautifully
matched teams of blooded horses was a daily amusement.
Every hotel provided stables for patrons who brought
their own horses and carriages with them. The favorite
drive was along the wide beach. Polished brass, glittering
silver or gold mounted harness made the equipages
striking. Summer residents who owned private mansions
also imported costly carriages and famous teams and
coachmen. Among the teams were thorougbreds from
Kentucky, Arabia, Virginia, Canada, and Russia. The
popular vehicles of the day included the landau, phaeton,
buggy, cabriolet, dog-cart, "T" cart, and barouche. As

the roads around the resort and into the countryside were gradually improved, there was even more incentive for importing horses and carriages for the summer season.

The luxurious carriages were well suited to the ladies' wide skirts. On the drives the ladies protected the pallor of their complexions with small parasols, creations of silk and lace with handles adjustable to any angle. Sun tan and freckles were looked on with horror in those days. The drives involved many courtly bows and hat tippings as the vehicles passed one another.

### PRESIDENTIAL GUESTS

In 1855 Franklin Pierce, the first President to visit the resort, arrived. Visitors came from far and wide to get their first glimpse of the President of the United States. Every vehicle that could be pressed into service was used to bring in people to attend the public reception.

President Grant made short sojourns in Cape May during four different seasons, although later he came to prefer Long Branch. His visits aroused intense excitement. At the time of his first arrival in 1869 many people regarded him as the greatest man living, and unusual preparations were made to receive him. It was planned that the Town Council of nine members would meet him at the railroad station, deliver an address of welcome, and extend to him the freedom of the city; but when they lined up to perform this function, they were such an insignificant-looking and ill-dressed lot a hotel proprietor, who was master of ceremonies, sent them home and substituted the nine best-looking guests in his house. One of the nine, in the role of mayor, delivered the welcome address with great éclat and presided at the banquet that evening. The genuine city fathers complained bitterly, but General Grant never knew the difference and the master of ceremonies had sufficient influence to keep the incident out of the papers.

In the summer of 1883 President Chester A. Arthur visited the Cape, arriving on the government steamer

*Dispatch.* He was honored by a banquet and a ball. He departed dramatically at midnight, when amid a great display of fireworks he was rowed to the *Dispatch* in a surfboat by the crew of the lifesaving station.

Another presidential guest was Benjamin Harrison, who arrived in 1889 to visit his Postmaster-General, John Wanamaker of Philadelphia, at his cottage on Cape May Point. With President Harrison came Secretary of State James G. Blaine and General William T. Sherman. In 1890 Wanamaker and some other friends gave Mrs. Harrison a summer cottage there, and the Harrison family occupied it for the seasons of 1890 and 1891. An executive officer was established at Congress Hall. An item appearing in the *New York Herald,* July 12, 1891, indicated the interest taken in every aspect of the President's life, "It is in his bathing suit, bare-legged, armed, and headed, that Mr. Harrison shows his improvements in physique to the best advantage."

Cape May felt the effects of the Civil War sharply and never regained its eminence as a resort of fashion, although its reputation was slow to die. The Southern planters and their families could no longer afford the extravagant living of pre-War days, had they wanted to go North for a vacation. The ravages of fire accelerated the decline, as the gay life of many a hotel ended in flames. On September 5, 1855, the Mount Vernon Hotel burned with a loss of six lives. The following year the Mansion House, built in 1832, was razed by fire. In 1869 a large portion of the village was destroyed in a fire, including the United States Hotel, the American House, and the Atlantic House. The Stockton Hotel built that year by the Pennsylvania Railroad at a cost of six hundred thousand dollars, burned in the most disastrous fire of Cape May's history in November, 1878. Thirty acres of ground were swept in a conflagration that destroyed more than half a million dollars' worth of property, including Congress Hall, the Columbia, seven other hotels, and about thirty private cottages. Congress Hall and the Columbia were rebuilt of brick, but the latter burned once more in 1889.

After the Civil War, Cape May was still described as "the watering place of the season," but by 1900 the observation was rightly made that it had lost its prestige and its preeminence among seashore resorts. After 1900 Cape May was known as a family resort.

Long Branch reached its height as a fashionable resort after Cape May had begun to decline. By 1860, when Paris dress designers came there to copy fashions acceptable to American society, it had definitely arrived. The advent of the Civil War upset Long Branch, but it revived when Mrs. Abraham Lincoln arrived for a visit. Her stay there almost coincided with the first Battle of Bull Run, and her visit proved of greater interest than the progress of the war. All along the beach, from every hotel, and in every dooryard the American flag floated in the breeze. A number of little girls, dressed in white, lined the path from her railroad car to the carriage, and a procession followed her from the depot to the hotel, despite her expressed desire for quiet. In addition to a round of social pleasures, the resort showed Mrs. Lincoln its latest technique in rescue work. All the countryside came to see the President's wife watch a demonstration of Newell's latest adaptation of the breeches buoy. Mrs. Lincoln stayed ten days.

After the War Long Branch acquired a reputation as a favorite resort for people prominent in the political and theatrical worlds. General Winfield Scott, hero of the Mexican War, summered regularly there for almost twenty years. A number of great stage players, including Edwin Forrest and Edwin Booth, stayed there for many seasons. By the 1870's, friends of the resort claimed it was more popular than its competitors, Cape May, Saratoga, or Newport.

The presence of President Grant was a great drawing card. George W. Childs, the wealthy publisher of the *Philadelphia Public Ledger* and owner of shore property, induced the President to come to Long Branch in 1869 after his Cape May visit. Grant was attracted by the resort's reputation for gaming and gaiety, and the opportunity it offered for vigorous riding and driving, and he soon expressed a liking for the place. A group of nearby Elberon residents, including Childs, George Pullman, and Moses Taylor, the New York financier, purchased a cottage there for him. For years the house was referred to as the "summer Capitol."

Grant found some aspects of the social life a bit trying and, according to Claude Bowers in *The Tragic Era*, when "dashing Phil Sheridan," the famous general, was there "cutting quite a figure with his dancing," Grant himself "cut a sorry figure." It was at such an event that Grant was quoted as saying, "Madam, I had rather storm a fort than attempt another dance."

Gambling was legal at Long Branch, and a certain percentage was reserved for the public treasury. Various clubs were started when out-of-town gamblers began to invade the resort in the late 1860's. The most elaborate was the Pennsylvania Club, over whose gaming room were two large domes, topped by gold weathervanes, characteristic features of many gambling places then. The interior was done in the sumptuous style of the mid-Victorian period with large paintings, mantles crowded with vases, massive horsehair furniture, thick carpets, and marble-topped tables. Grant was a frequent visitor to this club, and later so was President Chester A. Arthur, an indication of the tolerant public view of gambling. It was estimated that during an average season between five and ten million dollars were wagered there, either at roulette and faro, or cards and dice. There were other popular gambling places, among them the New York Club and an establishment on the second floor of the Mansion House.

In addition to the gambling houses, a major card at Long Branch was the nearby race track. Monmouth Park, about three miles from the resort between Oceanport and Eatontown, was begun in 1869 when two partners purchased 128 acres and laid out a half-mile trotting track. In 1870 they sold the property to the Long Branch and Seashore Improvement Company, which held its first race on July 4, 1870. The grandstand was described in the magazine *Turf, Field, and Farm* as seating several thousand people and as one of the most magnificent in the country. On the opening day purses and stakes were $31,000, an unusually large sum for those times. The mutuel pools had been imported from France, and these ran the odds up and greatly increased the number of betters. The gambling that accompanied the races at Monmouth Park drew the sporting crowd to Long Branch. Hotels realized the value of the race track and contributed purses and stakes. A new clientele now began to demand the finest in accommodations, and several new hotels were built. At the best hotels, rates averaged four dollars a day, American plan. This included a room and four meals: with breakfast at eight, dinner at two, tea at six, and supper at nine.

Every big hotel maintained a brass band which gave concerts on the lawn at train time and in the evening played for the "hops" and balls. The "hops" were relatively informal affairs and the balls elaborately planned events. Saturday was the day the large crowds arrived and that was the night of the main dance. On other nights dancing stopped at half-past ten, but on Saturday the party would often last until midnight. For those who did not dance there were always card games and concerts.

The main social artery was called Ocean Avenue, despite the fact that it was little more than a dirt road with gravel sidewalks. Afternoons at four, victorias and landaus rolled along the street, the occupants exchanging gossip and taking careful note of each other's dress and appointments. The livery of the drivers often equaled that of the prancing horses in gaudiness. More people strolled along the sidewalk. The Avenue took on the aspect of a race track at train-time in the late morning in the evening. If the guests did not care to join the promenade, they could drive to nearby Pleasure Bay for a clambake or occasionally a regatta. Pleasure Bay was located on the Shrewsbury River, and the wealthy kept their yachts there.

Long Branch had its piers as well as Atlantic City, but on the whole they were not as successful. The small Bath House Pier, built in 1828 and used for landing vessels from New York in calm weather, was later demolished by a storm. No new pier of any size was built until 1878 when one was constructed opposite the Ocean Hotel. It was six hundred feet long, made of tubular iron, and lined with benches and refreshment booths. Excursion boats from New York used it until it was washed away in a storm in 1881.

Grant's successor, Rutherford B. Hayes, also liked Long Branch and came often to the resort to preserve its reputation as the summer capital. President Hayes never acquired his own summer residence, but stayed at the smart Elberon Hotel. Considerably less dazzling than Grant, the sole contribution of President and Mrs. Hayes to the social scene was their presence. Hayes' successor, James A. Garfield, was more socially inclined, but Grant never welcomed him. Despite the two-term tradition, Grant had ardently sought the nomination in 1880 which Garfield had won. When the two men finally met, Grant was cool and aloof and they exchanged only a few words.

President Garfield's death at the resort brought it into the national limelight. Garfield was shot at the station in Washington on July 2, 1881, by a half-crazed, disappointed office seeker. He was taken to the White House, and two operations were performed on August 2 to remove the two bullets. The weather was intensely hot and the doctors suggested Garfield be taken to Long Branch, where he arrived September 6. His presence focused the eyes of the country on the resort, and more than a hundred newspapermen arrived to cover the story. On September 11 there were indications that blood poisoning had affected his right lung. On the eighteenth, the President suffered a relapse and died about ten o'clock that evening. His body lay in state, and long lines filed past. The body was then taken to Washington and later to its final resting place in Ohio.

Although Vice-President Chester A. Arthur had taken a summer home that season at Long Branch, he was in New York City at the time of Garfield's death. After taking the oath of office as President in his New York home, he left for Long Branch. Arthur continued to visit the place, but the fashionable people who had been coming there gradually began seeking other resorts, as the track and the casinos attracted increasing numbers of professional gamblers, sharpers, and confidence men. Grant remained a summer visitor until 1884, when his brokerage firm failed. Gradually more business men and theatrical people came to the resort, among them Lily Langtry, the famous "Jersey Lily," and later "Diamond Jim" Brady, who usually appeared with the glamorous Lillian Russell on his arm.

Increasingly stringent gambling laws were passed by the State Legislature, and in 1897 a constitutional amendment was adopted which forbade gambling or bookmaking. Horse racing itself was not outlawed thereby, but the prohibition of gambling brought about the same result. This marked the beginning of the end of an era for Long Branch. Saratoga started to reclaim the followers of the turf, just as Newport had earlier won back the ultra-fashionable people who had found Long Branch too flashy for their tastes. As the new century opened, Long Branch realized its future as a resort depended upon developing new attractions less liable to public disapproval.

### KEEPING THE SABBATH

In contrast to life at the fashionable places, life at the resorts which developed under the auspices of religious denominations was limited by a series of restrictions which seem unreasonable today. This was true of Ocean City at its inception and even more so of Ocean Grove, where the religious restrictions were continued into the twentieth century.

At Ocean City, in Cape May County, the three Methodist ministers who founded the resort set up many regulations through their Ocean City Association. They were especially desirous of keeping the Sabbath. On Sundays, in the earlier years of the resort, it was not permissible to launch a boat to the mainland, to drive a horse and buggy, or even to go in bathing. Within a few years, however, these restrictions were modified and, in later years, they were gradually discontinued.

At Ocean Grove, in Monmouth County, life was even more circumscribed. This resort, under the charter granted by the Legislature in 1870, remained a private association and did not become a municipality; hence its regulations were those any private club could make. The matter of Sunday bathing was one of the first to receive serious consideration by the Association, "lest," in the words of a critical contemporary account, "the lessons of purity imparted at the camp-meetings be forgotten under the influence of Neptune, whose bad reputation in mythology the Association was familiar with."

To clarify its position in the 1880's, a regulation was passed requesting "All respectable people . . . to discountenance the practice of the sexes in assuming attitudes on the sand that would be immoral at their city homes or elsewhere." It was added that if this rule was not observed, "It becomes the duty of the police to serve a small card on the offending person, and if the thing is repeated, the offender must be ordered from the beach."

It was chiefly in the regulations by which it protected the ends for which it was founded that Ocean Grove became most distinguished from the other resorts. In order to maintain control over the character of the population, lots were leased for 99 years with the privilege of renewal. The lease carried with it the full burdens of ownership in the way of taxes and the privileges of ownership, including the sale of the lease during satisfactory tenancy and fulfillment of the provision that no liquor be sold or any nuisances created on the

premises. No theatrical or like entertainment was allowed, nor any organ-grinder, pack peddler, scissors-
grinder, or push-cart vendor. The sale of tobacco was
strictly prohibited, and smoking was not permitted in the
neighborhood of the camp meeting grounds. Alcoholic
liquors were forbidden, under severe penalty, by special
act of the Legislature. This prohibition extended for a
statute mile from the limits of Ocean Grove Association,
which affected Asbury Park. No carriages were permitted
on the beach and no velocipedes or bicycles on the
plank-walks. No swearing was allowed in the boats on
Wesley Lake, though there were no suggestions as to
just how this could be enforced. No newspapers could
be sold on Sunday, nor, by agreement with the government of Asbury Park, within one block of the Asbury
end of the bridges.

The gates of the resort were closed at ten o'clock
every evening and all day on Sunday, when no one
could enter except by the bridges over Wesley Lake.
These were foot bridges, and thus no vehicle could
enter the resort on Sundays. No milk was distributed
that day and even physicians, though summoned on an
emergency, were required to go in on foot. They were
carefully watched and only those desiring to attend
services were allowed to cross. Persons were liable to a
fire of ten dollars if they crossed for any other purposes.
"Far-fetched as the comparison may seem," wrote a contemporary, "I cannot think of the lake and bridges
by which one enters this resort otherwise than of the
moat and drawbridges of some medieval fortified town
governed by an autocrat."

Dancing and card playing were frowned upon. In
this respect the attitude of members of the Association
was illustrated by an episode at the turn of the century.
A policeman was requiring a couple of young men to
desist from a game of cards. He was angrily told by
them that the Association leaders were "the most bigoted
set of men we ever heard of." To this the officer retorted,
"The association leaders pass no law requiring you to

come and after you have come, if you do not like it, there is nothing to compel you to stay."

The sanctity of the Sabbath was one of the fundamental principles upon which Ocean Grove was founded. In keeping with this idea it was felt that trains should not be allowed to stop on Sundays at the station, which was used jointly with Asbury Park. The matter was discussed with railroad officials in 1879 and, when the first passenger trains on Sunday were run south from Long Branch in 1881, no stop was made at the Asbury Park–Ocean Grove Station. Quite naturally, the citizens of Asbury Park protested, and recurring demands were made by them at the turn of the century that trains be allowed to stop at the Asbury Park–Ocean Grove Station. In 1910 a petition was sent from the Asbury Park Council to the newly created State Public Utilities Commission. The Commission, after a series of hearings, decided that public interest demanded that trains stop there on Sunday, and the railroad was ordered to begin such service on November 1, 1911. An appeal was taken by the Ocean Grove Association to the courts, but the Commission's decision was upheld.

During one season President Grant's mother and sister occupied a cottage near Wesley Lake, and Grant made frequent trips by carriage from Long Branch to visit them. Grant loved good horses, and Main Avenue, wide and straight, offered him an almost irresistible temptation to drive his fine team at full speed. The Chief of Police had to warn him against driving too fast more than once, but he testified proudly that the President always complied instantly, reining in his spirited bays to a decorous trot.

Once President Grant announced that he was coming to Sunday evening meeting to hear his pastor from Washington. The Association authorities were in a quandary. Since the President would drive down from Long Branch, the question arose, should he be required to get out of his carriage and walk into the Grove like any common man? Finally, the Secretary of the Association wrote him directly, and Grant rose to the occasion. "Enforce your rules," he replied. "When I come to Ocean Grove on Sunday, I will walk in like any other law-abiding citizen." And this he did.

Much of the activity of Ocean Grove centered around its huge Auditorium. By 1870 the site had been selected and a covered platform erected. Pine planks were used for seats. In 1874 a substantial frame building was raised, and in 1880 this was enlarged to cover nearly half an acre. Over eighty thousand dollars was subscribed for the building by those attending the camp meetings, and it was claimed that ten thousand people could worship there. Seats for a choir of five hundred were in full view of the congregation, whose seats were on a gentle incline so that each person could have a full view of the speaker.

During camp meeting, religious services were held almost continuously every day. A consecration meeting at quarter of six in the morning began the day. This was usually in charge of an officer of the Association and consisted of religious songs, testimonials, prayer, and altar service. At seven o'clock there were family prayers for transients who could not meet in the usual family service. This service was held in the Auditorium and lasted fifteen minutes. Every morning at nine o'clock the Holiness Meeting was held in the Tabernacle, with the reading of Scriptures, short expositions, hymns, religious testimony, and prayer. This lasted an hour. A young people's meeting was held at the same time in the Young People's Temple.

At half-past ten in the morning everyone gathered in the great Auditorium to listen to the sermon of the day. In the afternoon there was a service of prayer and song. A children's meeting was held in the Temple from half-past three to half-past four. This "aimed to impress the minds of children with the beauty of a religious life compared with one of worldliness and sin." A Twilight Service with special references to unconverted people was held either in the Tabernacle or Temple.

By 1900 the age of the automobile was at hand. The first appeared in Atlantic City in 1899, and its coming marked the beginning of a new era at the shore. In fact, until the democratization of the automobile in the 1920's, the horse continued to figure importantly in the lives of most shore people. A study of census figures indicates that the number of horses mounted steadily in the four shore counties throughout the nineteenth century. The number of horses reached its peak in 1910, as automobiles and trucks began to increase.

The shore had experienced remarkable development in the years between 1850 and 1900, but in the following decades it was to undergo even vaster changes.

# Part III

# THE AUTOMOBILE AGE
## SINCE 1900

# VII

## THE ERA OF THE
## HORSELESS CARRIAGE

---

The people received their first introduction to the
horseless carriage today when a family came slowly
into town mounted on an automobile. . . . The vehicle was driven by a small gasoline engine and
made unsteady progress. . . . If this is a fair sample
of the machine that many writers prophesy will
soon supersede the horse, then all we can have to
say is that noble animal has a long call on the auto.

A Bridgeton newspaper, 1899

By the turn of the century the gasoline-motor automobile
rumbled into the seashore area. Things would never be
quite the same again. In fact, this new means of transportation changed life even more than the advent of the
railroad half a century earlier. The earliest automotive
vehicles were the "electrics," powered by storage batteries, preceding the gasoline-driven cars. The first arrival
in Atlantic City, in the fall of 1899, was an imported
French electric car which aroused widespread interest.

At approximately the same time the "electrics" came
to Long Branch. The most talked-about car there was
one purchased by "Diamond Jim" Brady. To assure himself that he would always have a car ready to use,
Diamond Jim bought six electrics from a New York
salesman, who was requested at the same time to select
six good chauffeurs. Of the vehicles in his fleet, the
one that attracted the most attention at Long Branch
was the one constructed to his order. The salesman

recalled that Brady demanded that it be built like a brougham with a semicircular glass front that came down to the floor. "I don't care," Brady remarked, "so much about headlights on the road. What I figure on is a hundred concealed lights that will shine into the car." The automobile was then built to his specifications, and all aglow it rolled down Ocean Avenue displaying the beaming Diamond Jim and the lovely Lillian Russell. In the fall Brady shipped the car back to New York.

The chief limitation of the electrics was the short-lived battery. In this respect the vehicles proved most unsatisfactory. There were only a few places where the storage batteries could be charged, and if they went dead miles from an electric plant, it was necessary to hire a team, have it hitched to the car, and be hauled to the plant amid cutting comments from the bystanders, including the proverbial "Get a horse."

The gasoline-motored auto followed close on the tires of the "electrics" at the resorts. A short time after the advent of the French car in Atlantic City, two men there purchased a pair of Wintons, the "snappiest American-made job." With their one-cylinder motors they had a top speed of about ten miles an hour. Later the Winton Company developed a four-cylinder motor, and six more cars of that make were brought to the resort. All were steered by levers and could make the unheard-of speed of 40 miles an hour. To service the new cars the first garage was opened on South Carolina Avenue in 1900. By 1904, according to a display advertisement in the *Asbury Park Press* of July 18, shore residents could buy a Ford with two cylinders, "no vibration, and a speed of eight to thirty miles an hour." In this year the police of Atlantic City motorized their auto patrol to keep speeders in check and to bring disorderly persons into headquarters. The "Black Maria" was an electric—its principal job was to collect drunks. It stopped frequently for re-charging at the old electric plant on New York Avenue.

The first garage in Asbury Park was established in

1905 by C. R. Zacharias, whose first job was repairing a Locomobile. Zacharias was an outstanding example of keeping abreast of the changing times. In 1892 he was a leading figure in the Asbury Park Wheelmen's Club. In these years he helped build bicycle paths and was instrumental in getting Neptune Township to appropriate five hundred dollars for one in the later 1890's. In 1894 he procured a Columbia Bicycle, and at the turn of the century he purchased his first auto, an electric. His garage was successful, and by 1911 the local paper referred to him as the pioneer auto dealer on the Jersey coast.

The arrival of the automobile and truck caused a momentous shift in vocations, eliminating the blacksmith shops, the wheelwright shops, and the livery stables. The change was gradual but steady. Many livery stables built accommodations for storing autos and furnished taxi service. In 1905, for instance, a newspaper item from Atlantic City announced the recent construction, by the proprietor of a livery stable, of an eight thousand dollar building to store autos.

The motor car offered opportunities for a new type of recreation for shore visitors, "touring." At that time, "touring" was used to mean taking drives nearby. Early in the twentieth century items began to appear in local newspapers about guests pleasure-driving along the shore roads in their new automobiles. Three of these items, appearing in one August, 1904, issue of the Asbury Park paper, described the activities of tourists. One couple brought their famous "Yale" automobile with them and "toured" over the "beautiful drives and retreats" surrounding the city.

By this time special "tally-ho" autos, accommodating a large group, were offering drives along the shore. The Asbury Park newspaper of August 30, 1904, contained an account of one of the liveliest tally-ho parties of the season. The big machine left Ocean Grove at quarter-past three in the afternoon, amid the cheers of guests and neighbors, for Lakewood. The route taken passed through

Belmar and Point Pleasant, with return by way of Allaire, which was then called "the Deserted Village." Seventeen people took the trip and the item concluded by saying, "Words failed to express the delight of the party as they arrived home at 6:30 P.M. from their flying trip. . . . Refreshments were served on the automobile."

All the resorts along the shore felt the influence of the new vehicle. News items in the Atlantic City papers showed closer contacts with metropolitan Philadelphia. It was news when an automobile traveled from the city to the seashore. The *Atlantic Review* ran a headline on January 2, 1905, "Auto Trips Will Now Be Popular," over a story about a group who had come from Philadelphia in their "big Panhard car." In April the same paper declared a new record had been established by a man who drove from his home at Fifth and Poplar Streets in Philadelphia to Atlantic City in two hours and fifteen minutes. The vehicle was a sixty-horsepower car, and the roads were said to be in excellent shape. It was also announced that eight auto parties had arrived at Atlantic City on the previous day.

Even some New Yorkers were motoring to Atlantic City at this time.

In January, 1905, the same paper ran another headline, "From Gotham in a Touring Car," and the story described a fast run from New York to the shore made by a guest in his "powerful touring car." A few days later, it was chronicled, a party arrived from Philadelphia in their Mercedes and another from Haverford in their big Winton. Within a few years so many visitors were appearing at the shore in their automobiles that they no longer rated separate items.

In 1908 Long Branch introduced automobile races at its Elkwood Park. The local citizenry felt that there was enough excitement in watching cars tear along at fifty or sixty miles an hour to compensate for the absence of betting. The greatest attraction that season was a well advertised and well attended match between four of the fastest automobiles in the country, one of which was

Barney Oldfield's "Green Dragon." Two of the others were foreign, a Mercedes and a Renault; the fourth was a Packard.

In 1908 Atlantic City established an annual "Sociability Run" from Philadelphia to Atlantic City. The person who won this race in 1911 drove a Columbia and the time was 3 hours, 46 minutes, and 16 seconds for the 72.7 miles. This was before the construction of the pikes to the shore. The Sociability racers reported varying mishaps along the road, and some had had to turn back.

### DRIVING TO THE SHORE

By 1920 cars were a common sight, although the greater percentage of visitors to the shore still came by railroad. In a Fourth of July news story for 1922 it was announced that, while many visitors had come to Atlantic City by train, the outstanding feature of the crowds was the number who had arrived by automobile. Cars were parked on the avenues by the hundreds, and at least half of them bore what were called "foreign" license plates. Of these, most were from Pennsylvania, with New York second.

The early motorists in the shore area, as elsewhere, found many problems on the road. Throughout most of the first decade of the century automobiles were not equipped with windshields. If the owner wanted one, he had to pay quite a bit extra for it. If he got one, the only wiper was a chamois, and in a storm he had to stop frequently to wipe off the windshield. Drivers usually avoided night runs, since the acetylene-gas lights were weak. Gas for the headlamps was kept in brass tanks. The lights often refused to work when needed most. Few of the early vehicles had tops. If they did, the passengers had to get out and get them up when a sudden storm arose. There were no facilities for repairing tires, and a flat tire on the road was a major catastrophe. Usually a flat meant immediate repairs on the spot or the ruin of expensive casing or tube. When the engine refused to function, the blacksmith and the bicycle shop men knew little about its repair. For that matter, the owner often knew less than the repair man, and the latter could tinker all he wanted to and make any charge he wished.

The problem of procuring gasoline was often a pressing one. It cost only six to eight cents a gallon, since there was no tax on it, but there were no pumps either; it was poured from a five-gallon can. It was dispensed at grocery stores which stocked it for fuel in cooking stoves. The motorist usually carried a spare can of gasoline; if he ran out of fuel, he often had to walk miles to get more. On holiday weekends the shortage of gasoline sometimes became acute at the shore resorts. At Asbury Park, for instance, the Fourth of July in 1904 brought unexpected demands. To make matters worse, a railroad car of gasoline, already a week overdue, failed to arrive. Automobilists found themselves in straits because of the scarcity of fuel and offered ridiculously high prices for it. One chauffeur was said to have gone into a local grocery store and offered a dollar a gallon for it. The Zacharias garage sent to Red Bank and got a wagon-load of ten barrels.

One of the most difficult problems arose in passing an excitable horse. Horses frightened by cars caused many serious accidents. A typical one was described in the *Asbury Park Press* in August, 1904. A group of visitors were driving across Deal Lake Bridge toward Long Branch when a large automobile frightened their horse, which swerved to one side, throwing the occupants from the carriage and breaking the front wheels of the vehicle. The animal, mad with fright, kicked himself loose from the trap and tore down the main boulevard. The owner of the car stopped and assisted the injured, who fortunately were not seriously hurt.

As the number of automobiles on the road increased, curbing their speed was advocated. A correspondent of a local paper in 1904 suggested that the towns between Camden and Atlantic City arm their constables with guns to be used in puncturing the tires and machinery of the offending vehicles. A year later an Atlantic City newspaper announced that any constable or police officer was authorized to arrest without warrant any person driving a motor vehicle contrary to the law. In 1906 the state passed a motor law limiting the speed to ten miles an hour on curves. On the open road a speed of 20 miles was allowed.

Not only did automobiles cause accidents by frightening horses, but they themselves became involved in accidents brought on by speeds too great for roads built for horses and buggies. One of the first speeding accidents was chronicled in August, 1904, in the Asbury Park paper. A touring car belonging to a New York lawyer went out of control while going at a "rapid rate" at Belmar. It was said to have been going 40 miles an hour when it toppled over a five-foot embankment on the curve near the Shark River Bridge. Fortunately, no one was killed. Few shore county bridges were built to bear up under such fast passage.

The problem of fees for automobiles arose early in the century. At first car owners registered at the office of the chief official of their town who sent the registration to Trenton for filing. No license plates were issued. The State issued a license card, and the owner furnished his own tag. Sometimes it was a leather belt on which were hung metal numerals of the same type as those used for house numbers. In 1906 the Legislature created the Motor Vehicle Department, and in that year 13,759 automobiles were registered in New Jersey, and $67,973 in fees was collected. Autos equipped with engines up to thirty horsepower were rated at three dollars a year, and those over thirty at five dollars.

By 1911, when more out-of-state cars began to appear at the seashore, the problem of reciprocity concerning state licensing arose. At that time Pennsylvania and Delaware refused to reciprocate, and New Jersey retaliated by charging motorists from those states a fifteen-dollar license fee. Atlantic City hotel men were the first to complain to the State Commissioner of Motor Vehicles, for they feared that motorists from those states would stay out of New Jersey rather than pay the fee. Resort authorities from Long Branch, Asbury Park, Wildwood, and Cape May joined a delegation from Atlantic City at Trenton for a grievance meeting, at which Governor Woodrow Wilson promised to remedy the situation. Eventually reciprocity was achieved.

One problem the automobile public faced from the start was the need for better roads. None had been built to meet the demands of the new vehicle. Gravel was the chief surface material, and in many shore areas a considerable amount of clay was mixed with the gravel. In winter the roads soon rutted and froze and made very rough going. When they thawed out in the spring they seemed to be bottomless.

More than any other form of transportation, from ox to airplane, the automobile provided the greatest impetus to the improvement of highways. As early as 1907 one shore newspaper expressed the belief that the new auto owners would be a strong force for road improvement.

For the shore areas in Cape May and Atlantic Counties, of greatest importance was the completion of two main arteries, the White Horse Pike and the Black Horse Pike, both of which provided motor access from Philadelphia and Camden. By 1898, thanks to some extent to the efforts of the bicyclists, the White Horse Pike had been partially graveled by county authorities, and by 1904 it was referred to as a modern Appian Way. In 1919 a new road was built across the salt meadows from Absecon which allowed the Pike to run directly into Atlantic City, but it was not until 1921 that the final stretch was hard surfaced.

The need for another route to the seashore was heightened in 1926 by the completion of the Delaware River Bridge (later called the Benjamin Franklin Bridge) between Camden and Philadelphia, eliminating the need to rely on the ferries. Traffic over the bridge increased steadily, and a decade later ten and a half million vehicles used it while the ferries carried about two and a half million vehicles annually.

The Black Horse Pike route was plotted in 1928 through Williamstown and Pleasantville, and it was finally opened to shore traffic in 1932. With the opening in May, 1957, of the Walt Whitman Bridge and the East-West Freeway connecting with the Black Horse Pike, that roadway became overburdened with traffic, and in 1962 a new Authority, discussed below, was set up to construct a toll expressway from the end of the East-West Freeway to Atlantic City.

Closer connection between the sea islands was inaugurated with the completion in the 1930's of the Longport–Ocean City Bridge, the initial link in the Ocean Drive. The Ocean City paper marveled in 1939 at the improved facilities. In 1912 a trip to Atlantic City by motor car was considered a major event in the life of an Ocean City resident. It meant that two hours would be spent traveling over graveled roads, rutted and hard on both man and machine. After the construction of the new Somers Point–Ocean City Bridge the trip took 25 minutes by the mainland route, but over the Ocean City–Longport toll bridge it took only 15 minutes. In the following decade the Ocean Drive was completed southward with the construction of a new toll bridge to replace an old wooden one over Corson's Inlet and the building of the three new toll bridges. One over Townsend's Inlet connected Sea Isle City with Avalon; another over Hereford Inlet joined Stone Harbor with Anglesea and North Wildwood; while the third, over Cold Spring Harbor, united Two-Mile Beach with Cold Spring and West Cape May.

The two northern shore counties also benefited by the road improvement program. The first gravel road in Ocean County was built by the Board of Freeholders in 1904 to connect Lakewood with Point Pleasant. Later improved roads were built the length of Long Beach Island, from Beach Haven to Barnegat Inlet, and on Island Beach north of the Inlet from Seaside Park to

Manasquan Inlet. In June, 1914, an automobile bridge was opened connecting Long Beach Island with Manahawkin on the mainland. It was built by private capital as a toll bridge. Long Beach resorts were now accessible by automobile all the way to Beach Haven. Within ten years after the bridge was opened, the island's summer population increased more than it had in the forty previous years. Later the State took over the bridge, freed it from toll, and improved it. By 1935 the last few miles of concrete were laid for a direct route from Philadelphia to the resorts on the island.

In the mid-twenties Ocean and Monmouth County residents began a campaign to persuade the State to build a hard-surfaced road connecting Asbury Park with the Camden-Philadelphia area. The Navy, with its Naval Air Station at Lakehurst, was also anxious to have good communications with Philadelphia. The road was finished in the mid-thirties.

Island Beach to the north was easier to get to after a bridge was built from north of the mouth of Toms River across shallow Barnegat Bay to Seaside Heights. Called the Barnegat Bay Bridge, it became a part of the State highway system in 1921.

A wide network of improved roads developed in the Monmouth County shore area, especially connections with urban north Jersey and New York. In 1930 work was begun on a long-sought State road from Keyport along the shore of Raritan Bay to Highland Beach on the Atlantic, including a new bridge over the Shrewsbury River at Highlands, which served the northern tier of towns in the County. The year 1936 marked the completion of the Victory Bridge across the mouth of the Raritan, which provided a bypass for Perth Amboy and eliminated a bottle-neck at the Woodbridge Circle. Later, the Edison Bridge, called a "superspan over the Raritan" by a local paper, further facilitated the traffic flow from New York.

Of major importance to the growth of the shore was the construction in the 1950's of the 173-mile Garden

State Parkway, which became the main route from the north to all seashore resorts. Its southern terminus is near Cape May City. Serving Cape May, Atlantic, Ocean, and Monmouth Counties, it gives access to all shore locations for the populous north Jersey counties and the New York metropolitan area. Construction was begun in 1952 and completed in 1955 except for one missing link, over Great Egg Harbor near Ocean City, which was forged in 1956. The nine-mile feeder road to join the Parkway with the New York State Thruway was finished in 1957. The Authority administering the road pays its debts and costs with tolls and other revenues.

The Parkway is a divided highway. The accident rate ranks well below that for New Jersey highways collectively as well as that for the nation's roads. Its center island ranges up to six hundred feet in width and contains numerous picnic areas, service locations, and heavily wooded pinelands. By 1963, 91 interchanges had been provided, including 124 entrance ramps and 122 exits. A new interchange was planned, to be completed in 1964, at Pleasantville, to link the Parkway with the proposed Atlantic City Expressway. This 44-mile toll road was authorized by the 1962 Legislature as a connection between the North-South Freeway in Camden County and Atlantic City, thus providing quicker access to the shore from the Philadelphia-Camden metropolitan area. It was estimated that the Expressway link to the Parkway would provide, in its first year of operation, an additional four hundred ten thousand dollars in tolls from the lightly-traveled southern section of the Parkway between Ocean and Cape May Counties.

The highway improvements spelled diminished returns for the railroads, which gradually found themselves unable to compete with the new form of transportation. Even as early as 1923 it was declared that more traffic was coming into the seashore area by automobiles than by railroad. My mid-century most of the summer trade arrived by car. A traffic count at the approaches to Atlantic City at the height of the summer season, the third week in August, 1950, revealed that seventy-five thousand autos had entered the city in the 48 hours from Friday midnight to Sunday midnight. The heaviest travel was on the White Horse Pike, via Absecon Boulevard.

The railroads gradually began to cut services on the main lines and to drop the shore spur lines. One of the first to be given up was a road operated from Beach Haven north to Barnegat Inlet, on Long Beach, which was abandoned in 1923. Later small stations were closed and other spur lines abandoned. In 1934, for example, the station at Como on the Monmouth County shore, a landmark for nearly forty-five years, was officially closed by the New York and Long Branch Railroad. In the 1940's further retrenchment took place; e.g., in 1945 the railroad from Long Branch to Sandy Hook, incorporated in 1863, was abandoned.

In Atlantic and Cape May Counties the railroads had to make similar readjustments to modern conditions. The effect of carrier competition was heightened by the depression, with the result that plans were made for consolidation of the two rival lines serving these Counties, the Reading and the Pennsylvania. The State Board of Public Utility Commissioners, following an intensive investigation, reported in 1931 that the plan was feasible. The merger was effected in 1933–1934 under the title of the Pennsylvania-Reading Seashore Lines. Branch lines that once competed were torn up, and only one line into a resort remained. The line that entered Atlantic City from Absecon was continued, but the old Narrow Gauge route of the Reading that came in by Pleasantville was given up. At Cape May, the merger was followed by tearing up the Pennsylvania's tracks and the demolition of Grant Street Station; only one main route to Cape May from Camden was retained, by way of Winslow Junction. Efforts of the consolidated lines to substitute bus transportation for steam trains during the winter season resulted in such stiff opposition that the idea was given up temporarily.

The railroad authorities firmly resisted the demands

for improvement and increase in commutation facilities. In 1947, Wildwood residents attacked the road's management, pleaded for the retention of an all-year-round Bridge Train direct into Philadelphia, and told the officials that they were riding in "glorified box cars with every window jammed closed and the doors between the cars closed to keep out dirt." The general manager of the Pennsylvania-Reading Seashore Lines replied that, even if the company were to operate modern de luxe cars, he did not believe it could increase its business ten per-cent. "We have made thorough studies," he went on, "and regardless of train service, the people want their car at the shore." Further retrenchment has occurred in the subsequent sixteen years.

The automobile had greatly quickened the pulse of life at the seashore in the twentieth century. New forms of diversion emerged and new problems were to be faced, and in one critical storm in 1962 the seashore lost much of its beach.

# VIII

## TWENTIETH CENTURY
## DIVERSIONS AND PROBLEMS

---

> The Easter Parade at the Queen of Resorts . . . was
> gorgeous and beautiful. . . . It was a superb day,
> . . . with fine toggery and Easter hats and bonnets.
> By noon, the walk was filled to overflowing, . . .
> and such a parade! Every color of the rainbow was
> there. Masculinity was also gorgeously robed.
> An Atlantic City newspaper, 1905

In the twentieth century, new forms of recreation became popular with shore visitors and residents. Moving
pictures appeared in the first decade of the century. A
1905 advertisement in an Atlantic City newspaper urged
readers to view a "masterpiece of animated photog-
raphy," depicting a "realistic stagecoach hold-up and
hand-to-hand pistol fight." The first film shown in Long
Branch portrayed firemen and a three-alarm fire. It was
exhibited in a small room in the entrance building of the
Iron Pier. In 1909, a "Nickelette Theatre" there began to
show one-reel comedies and melodramas, and in the same
year the West End Bathing Pavilion was transformed
into the Bluff Theatre, the only motion picture house on
the boardwalk. With the coming of television in the mid-
century years, however, interest in the movies declined,
despite the fact that television reception along much of
the seashore was not clear unless the householder had an
extra-high antenna built from the ridgepole of his roof,
or paid a monthly charge to have the picture "piped in."

The mailing of souvenir postcards of the "wish-you-
were-here" type became popular with all visitors, who

bought them to send to friends sweltering in the city. The custom had its beginnings in the last years of the nineteenth century. The first souvenir postcards at the seashore and, it was claimed, in the whole United States, were introduced at Atlantic City in 1895 by a German-American who had visited her childhood home on the Rhine that year and brought back an assortment of picture postcards then on sale in Germany. Her husband conceived the idea of introducing the souvenir card to this country. He had about ten thousand cards printed in colors, expecting that they would be purchased by the hotels and business people in Atlantic City for advertising purposes. The greater portion of the printing was left on his hands, and eventually he began to sell them to the public at bargain prices. Within a few seasons visitors accepted the idea and souvenir cards sold in increasing numbers.

The fad spread; in 1906 a total of one and a half million souvenir cards passed through the Atlantic City Post Office during the month of August alone. The craze changed the pattern of stamp sales in the local office. Previously two-cent stamps (then used for letters) had accounted for the largest proportion of business, but now they sold scarcely more than one-fifth of the number of one-cent stamps sold. The post office reported that it had no trouble in canceling the stamps on ordinary postcards, but the leather "cards" and other novelties caused no end of difficulties, and had to be canceled by hand.

## BOARDWALK TRANSPORTATION

Among the more popular diversions, particularly on Atlantic City's Boardwalk, were the rolling chair and the annual Easter Parade. The rolling chair was first used in 1876 at Philadelphia's Centennial Exposition to take visitors over the extensive grounds. It was brought to the shore by an Atlantic City hardware dealer who rented it to invalids. In 1887 he procured a number of them to rent out for pleasure, complete with "pushers." (At that time the word "pusher" had no narcotic connotation.)

As the new type of vehicle increased in popularity, the number of chairs on the Boardwalk multiplied. By 1899 the rolling chair had become essential to the life of the resort. On pleasant Sundays hundreds of them could be seen "advancing, passing, and receding into the throng, traveling four miles an hour." Many of them were constructed of basketwork, which was described by an enthusiast as glowing "richly under its varnish" and as having "a swan's neck prow rising well in front." The passenger was well covered with warm fur-robes in the winter; in spring and fall he was provided with brightly-colored light blankets. Flat Japanese umbrellas were rigged above for shade. "When you have seen a pretty girl thus inframed, her lovely eyes drowsing in calm content, you have looked upon the finest picture you ever saw," concluded an 1899 account.

The rolling chair gave the Boardwalk its first traffic problem. Scores of complaints were made about the carelessness of the pushers. In 1905 the mayor was nearly "floored" by a chair bearing a two hundred-pound woman. The City Council thereupon ordered a ten-man patrol of policemen to direct rolling-chair traffic on Sundays. Although the patrol was reported as having acted promptly at every sign of congestion, conditions did not show much improvement, and soon the Council enacted a new ordinance requiring the chairs to keep to the middle of the walk, under penalty of a $25 fine.

That year the vehicle became the subject of a popular song entitled "Why Don't You Try," or the "Rolling Chair Song," the first stanza of which began, "Did you ever see a maiden in a little rolling-chair?" A few years later the walk itself became the locale of a song entitled "Moonlight on the Boardwalk," which included these sentimental lines:

Honey, you make me do what you know I oughtn't to.
　Oh, when it is moonlight, down on the Boardwalk,
My dearie, that's where I'll be,
　And everytime it's moonlight, then it's spoon-night,
Honey, wait for me.

In the twenties, Irving Berlin became so inspired while chair-borne, it is claimed, that he hopped out, hurried back to his hotel, and dashed off "All Alone."

Following World War II, the increasing numbers of electrically operated "chairmobiles" on the Boardwalk raised a number of protests. In 1948, an ordinance permitting the licensing of one hundred such chairs was passed. The Chamber of Commerce branded motor chairs a "walk menace" and one editorial writer queried:

Must we surrender our . . . World Famous Boardwalk to the Lilliputian electric edition of Uncle Henry's gasoline buggy? Shall we stand idly by while the disciples of speed substitute their chairmobile for our man-propelled, leisurely moving temples of contentment that represent to weary humans the very essence of relaxation and rest? Shall the chairpushers be forced to join the ranks of the unemployed, like Old Dobbin?

The electrically operated chairs, however, remained licensed, but their speed was limited to four miles an hour, and they were not permitted to carry bells, horns, or other noise-making devices.

### EASTER BONNETS

Rolling chairs were in heavy demand on certain special days, one of which was the annual Easter Parade, which by the turn of the century was increasingly popular. In 1905 one Easter Monday headline in an Atlantic City newspaper claimed: "Easter Sunday's Parade Glorious Spectacle, 100,000 Visitors March in Review on the Board Walk, Auto Parties Came From Many Cities, Railroads Never Had Such Crowds."

The main attraction, naturally, was what was worn by the ladies. In 1902, the local newspaper reported that hats were "mostly broad-brimmed, . . . trimmed with large roses and almost covered with chiffon and violets." By 1905 another trend was evident. The "waving plumes and lace of the hats," noted the paper, "suggest an exaggerated flower bed." Especially conspicuous were those of "glaring green," set off by "parasols of radiant colors."

By 1910 "baby doll" fashions predominated. "Certainly," commented the newspaper that year, "nothing ever made the young girl look sweeter . . . than the simple bonnet with a blue ribbon on it." By 1913 hats were "growing smaller" and a new note was injected with the daring "slash skirts."

The event became even more popular. In 1938, the "glamorous crowd for the colorful Easter Parade" was estimated as four hundred thousand. By 1941, attendance had increased to approximately half a million, an all-time record. Two years later the paper noted that the war had given "no fatal blow" to the Easter Parade. During the 1941 Easter weekend, banking houses at Atlantic City took in $1,502,245 in deposits; $1,614,882 in 1942; and $1,563,679 in 1943. Restaurants and rooming houses and those hotels not taken over by the Federal Government for wartime training were especially busy.

### BEAUTIES AND BABIES

One of the unusual features of resort life in the twentieth century was the attention and publicity given to baby parades, beauty pageants, the "Miss America" and "Mrs. America" competitions. The most publicized of these events was the Atlantic City Beauty Pageant which evolved into the "Miss Amercia" contest.

Inspired by Florenz Ziegfeld's contemporary efforts in "Glorifying the American Girl," local citizens had urged that the resort sponsor a nationwide beauty pageant, claiming it would focus attention on the resort and prolong the season beyond Labor Day. So the first pageant was held in Atlantic City in 1921; the accent was on good looks, pure and simple. In the years following, talent requirements were added so that the winner would be more "representative" and capable of fulfilling the lucrative personal-appearance tour that marked the year of her reign.

The pageant became larger each year until 1927, when a collapsing real estate boom caused the contest to be abandoned temporarily. It was revived in 1933, but the affair was put on without the backing of the Chamber of Commerce or the hotels, and it ran into financial difficulties. In 1935 the program was restored on a firm basis with the whole resort behind it. The "bathing-beauty" ideal was gone, and the search was for America's most typical girl, who was required to have charm, poise, and talent.

In 1940 the title of the event was changed to the "Miss America Pageant," and a few years later an intricate point system was evolved to select the winner. Points were earned in various events, with some consideration given to the well-proportioned figure, but also to voice and diction, intellect, wholesomeness, disposition and general culture, special talents, and personality. In the late forties, scholarships were contributed for the winner and fifteen other finalists. The contest had widespread ramifications. It was estimated that, for every "Miss America" crowned at the resort ten thousand girls competed in a thousand contests on the local and state levels which preceded the national contest.

Long before the beauty pageant was introduced at Atlantic City, the Monmouth County shore sponsored baby parades. The first of a series was held at Asbury Park in 1890. By 1910 the parade had become an established event. The preceding year it had been witnessed by one hundred thousand people. Various roles were portrayed by the children, among them Little Bo-Peep, Red Riding Hood, Cupid, and Puck. There were a number of Indian groups; express wagons were bedecked to convey allegorical ideas. In the words of the *Asbury Park Press,* "Go-carts were buried in flowers and set with infantile jewels."

During the depression and throughout the war years the baby parade was allowed to lapse, but it was revived in 1946. By 1948, however, another carnival phase commanded precedence and by mid-century had swallowed up the baby parade. If Atlantic City could sponsor a "Miss America" contest, Asbury Park could inaugurate a "Mrs. America" competition. As in the Atlantic City contest, by the end of the forties "Mrs. America" was no longer judged and selected on pulchritude alone; home-making abilities were also weighed. In 1950, the winner showed samples of her crocheting, won a floor-sweeping contest, and was required to cook some dish under observation by the judges. Declining interest and problems of sponsorship, however, brought changes, and by the mid-fifties the event was moved out of the State.

## DECENT OR DARING

From the very beginning of seashore resorts, public officials had worried about what constituted proper bathing attire, and they fought a stubborn but losing battle to enforce regulations which were always lagging behind public opinion. In 1878 the Atlantic City governing board issued an ordinance making it unlawful for any person "to bathe in the surf . . . except such person be so clothed as to prevent the indecent exposure of the body." To prevent "indecent exposure" at that time, bathers had to be completely covered from the neck down.

Bathing costumes at the turn of the century were almost as cumbersome as they had been twenty-five years before. Women's bathing suits were shorter and had short sleeves, but stockings were still thought necessary, and only the bather's face and lower arms were exposed. In the succeeding years, however, the suits became a bit more "daring"each year. The women's skirts shrank inch by inch until they were finally discarded. The men's trouser legs grew shorter and shorter until they were well above the knee. By 1924 Atlantic City authorities decided they might as well legalize an accepted situation; it was announced that "stockingless women and one-piece bathing suits" would be allowed on the beach. The bathing suit continued to be ruled off the Boardwalk, however. In the next decade police were baffled by women's "play-suits," which could not be banished since they were not bathing suits, but they covered little more of the wearer's anatomy than a bathing costume.

Next, authorities faced with determination the problem presented by men's topless suits. Those who wore them were called "beach nudists." In 1935 at Atlantic City 25 "semi-nude men bathers" were fined one dollar each for being nude to the waist. The newspaper reporting the incident referred to them as the "Tarzans of the Beach." In 1938, 24 "beach nudists" were taken to police headquarters in a patrol wagon. Despite this fact, men bathers continued to appear on the beach clad only in trunks. This mode of dress became increasingly accepted after the outbreak of World War II and its attendant shortages of wool and other fabrics. Finally, in 1941, Atlantic City officials gave in and decreed that topless suits for men would be allowed.

### THE MOSQUITO PEST

Another problem against which authorities waged a more successful battle was the "pestiferous" mosquito, long the bane of existence to shore residents and visitors. A letter from Atlantic City, published in a Philadelphia paper on August 11, 1858, complained that there was no peace in the place because of the mosquitoes. Smudges were lighted in front of houses to drive them off, but the blinding and dirty smoke was itself a nuisance. Children scratched the swollen bites on their limbs and faces, and excursionists urged train conductors to start homeward ahead of schedule. Efforts were made to have the breeding holes filled and graded, but nearby marshes remained. New Jersey became so widely known for its mosquitoes that in 1899 it was made the subject of an instrumental piece for the piano; the music was called "The Mosquitoes' Parade, a Jersey Review," and the subtitle explained that it simulated "the song and motions and bite of the Jersey 'skeeter.'"

In the twentieth century more effective measures were devised to control the pest. Drainage ditches, built by the State, criss-crossed the salt marshes, and by 1912 forty thousand acres of salt marsh from Secaucus in Hudson County to Barnegat in Ocean County had been ditched for drainage. The project later was extended farther south, but results were often disappointing. Heavy rains brought out a flood of salt-marsh mosquitoes despite ditching. But further ditching helped; by the mid-thirties over fifteen hundred miles of ditches had been constructed in Ocean County alone. This brought considerable improvement. In the late forties, other weapons were used, including spraying with DDT by airplane. The dusting planes flew from 15 to 25 feet above the marshland three times a season. By the 1950's, however, some question arose concerning the continued efficacy of DDT for mosquito control. One authority pointed out in 1952 that mosquitoes of the 1951 season were several times harder to kill than were their ancestors when the chemical was first used. Resistance had been built up. He recommended that more emphasis be placed on permanent mosquito control work in the marshes, such as drainage and filling, and less on chemicals. Even the lowly mosquito had learned to develop an armor in times of war.

### HORSE RACING AND FISHING

An oldtime form of amusement returned in the 1940's when large race tracks were built in Monmouth and Atlantic Counties. The racing center in Monmouth County had a long history behind it. After approval of a constitutional referendum in June, 1939, which allowed parimutuel betting on hore races, the Legislature established the State Racing Commission. In November, 1945, this body sanctioned the building of a race track near old Monmouth Park at Oceanport, just outside of Long Branch. The race track and grandstand were constructed in 1946. The Atlantic City race track was also opened in 1946 on the site of the former Atlantic Pines Golf Club, about twenty miles from the city. Both were well attended.

Fishing was one of the main attractions of a shore vacation in this period as it had been in the previous century. Since automobiles made it possible to get to the shore in a couple of hours, daily chartered-boat excursions became increasingly popular. Many residents made a livelihood from fishing, some by commercial fishing and other by catering to sportsmen.

In Monmouth County, Shark River was a favorite resort for boating and fishing parties; striped bass were the attraction for fishermen there. The river also furnished fish and soft shell crabs for the New York market. About 1900 the Federal Government built a jetty at the mouth of the river to protect it from shifting sands. A little farther south the Manasquan River was fished for striped bass, blue fish, and weakfish; crabs were plentiful.

It was Ocean County, however, which was best known for fishing, and also for gunning. Barnegat Bay was a feeding ground for wild fowl, and the pines region, with its creeks and swamps and ponds, afforded them refuge and security. In the latter part of the nineteenth century and the early years of the twentieth, all the villages along the main shore of Barnegat Bay and Little Egg Harbor were host to sportsmen at different seasons. Large numbers of anglers gathered at Forked River, where there were four hotels, and at Waretown and Barnegat, with two hotels each. Toms River, Manahawkin, West Creek, and Tuckerton also entertained guests who came for fishing and gunning. From these villages hundreds of catboats took the anglers out on Barnegat Bay and Little Egg Harbor Bay. In winter many boats were engaged to take out gunners from their headquarters in the mainshore towns. At Long Beach surf casting for big game fish was introduced in 1907. The sport grew in popularity.

Many people fished from their own boats, which included all types from rowboat to schooner to motor yacht. Others hired boats by the day or week and fished under the competent guidance of local captains who knew the waters and the best fishing grounds. During the early years of the century the method of fishing gradually changed from the bamboo pole and drop-line to high-quality rods and reels. Sportsmen were now provided with sinkers from one-half ounce to three ounces, graduated by the quarter-ounce, which made it possible to feel the bottom at intervals and keep the bait in constant motion, especially important for taking the big weakfish.

SAILING

Sailing, like fishing, had long been a popular form of recreation along the shore. All sections of the coast enjoyed spring, summer, and fall sailing on the bays between the sea islands and the mainland. A number of yacht clubs had been established by 1900, one of the oldest of which was the Beach Haven Yacht Club on Long Beach Island which dated from 1880. The Meadow Yacht Club at Sea Bright was incorporated in 1895, and by 1903 races were being held every Saturday afternoon. Two boat clubs were functioning at Red Bank by 1902. The Monmouth Boat Club, composed of Red Bank residents and summer visitors, owned a clubhouse on the river front which was open from April to November and later for the iceboat season. The other, the Red Bank Yacht Club, made up chiefly of summer residents, owned a floating clubhouse anchored near the Middletown shore opposite Red Bank. Its members held sailing and motorboat races every Saturday during the summer season, with regattas on the Fourth of July and Labor Day. The South Shrewsbury Ice Boat and Yacht Club was organized at Long Branch in 1896, the first in that city. Later in the 20th century the Shrewsbury Handicap Sailing Association, established in 1936, sponsored sailboat racing on the Shrewsbury River. During its first season an average of twenty-five boats sailed in races every Saturday afternoon throughout the summer.

The bays behind Long Beach in Ocean County were considered especially good for sailing, racing, or yachting. By 1936 there were several yacht clubs on the island. The largest was at Beach Haven where the Little Egg Harbor Yacht Club had nearly two hundred members, mostly summer residents owning pleasure craft.

The protected waters between the sea islands and the New Jersey coast formed a natural route for small craft.

They could proceed with comparative safety along most of the Jersey shore by using the Intracoastal Waterway, which provided an inland route from Bay Head at the northern end of Barnegat Bay to Cape May, serving the Ocean, Atlantic, and Cape May County shores. It was begun by the state in 1908, and by 1915 a 111-mile channel had been opened through the tidal bays and sounds that separated the sea islands from the mainland. The depth for most of the route was six feet, but there were many places where the water was not that deep at low tide. The route was well buoyed and marked, and even amateur yachtsmen had little difficulty in navigating it, despite the 26 drawbridges.

In the mid-twenties the State, with Federal aid, extended an eight-foot channel from Bay Head into the Manasquan River Inlet. Since the southern section of the Monmouth County shore had no barrier sea islands, there was no inland waterway from this point north to Sandy Hook, a distance of 28 miles. The Federal Government did what it could by building two stone jetties at the ocean entrance of Barnegat Inlet and dredging a channel eight feet deep across the flats of Barnegat Bay to connect with the Intracoastal Waterway.

In 1942 in World War II, the Federal Government built the Cape May Canal from the Intracoastal Waterway into Delaware Bay, about three and a half miles above Cape May Point. This provided a safe and shorter route by which small craft could avoid the dangerous tide rips encountered in rounding Cape May Point. The canal was about four miles long, twelve feet deep, and one hundred feet wide. In 1945 it was proposed that the Federal Government take over the operation of the entire Intracoastal Waterway and deepen it to twelve feet to keep small craft and barges from possible submarine attacks in coastal waters. It was not until 1954, however, that the New Jersey portion of the Intracoastal Waterway was formally handed over by the State, leaving just one gap, from Manasquan River to Sandy Hook Bay.

A new form of enterprise developed in the fifties, the

marina. One of the largest was the Atlantic City State Marina, started in 1954, with city and State sharing the costs. By 1962 a tenth and final pier had been built, at an overall cost of approximately two million dollars. In addition to providing docking facilities for craft from the area, it also played host to two thousand transient yachts with home ports from Canada to Florida. Gradually it became the headquarters of most boating and fishing activities in the area. Reached by a divided highway from the White Horse Pike, it provided parking for two hundred cars. By 1962 other marinas had been constructed at New Gretna, Bass River, Cedar Point at Toms River, Island Heights, and Cape Island at Cape May. All types of facilities were offered by the new establishments. Some provided service to boats with outboard motors. All had restaurants and gasoline pumps; some planned swimming pools, tennis courts, and motels.

As more shore areas were built up with hotels and private cottages, few places remained for the public use. When the State legislators finally began to realize the need for State parks along the ocean front, it was found that little of the area remained open for purchase. In 1926 the Legislature passed an act to provide for the location, selection, and management of lands bordering on the Atlantic Ocean for State parks, in order "to preserve and make accessible to the public the natural conditions of the virgin sand dunes of the New Jersey Coast."

By mid-century a few shore parks had been created. On July 9, 1951, the State took over Barnegat Light at Barnegat Inlet, from the Federal Government and set the comparatively small area up as a State Park, which was later somewhat enlarged. In 1950 negotiations were started to acquire Sandy Hook from the Federal Government, which no longer felt the need to keep up the coast artillery post at Fort Hancock. Tentative plans were made for converting the six-mile-long peninsula into a park modeled after Jones Beach on Long Island, with both ocean and bay beaches. The increasing seriousness of the Korean War and the "Cold War" and the enlarged military security program forced a revision of the plans. Finally, in 1961, the Federal Government decided it would be safe to lease 460 acres of the post; and in July, 1962, Sandy Hook State Park was opened to the public.

The Park was less than a mile across at its widest point and about one hundred fifty yards at its narrowest. For administrative purposes it was divided into three sections. The surf-fishing area was north of the entrance gate for a distance of one and a half miles, with bay fishing across the peninsula, extending three-fourths of a mile. The ocean bathing section centered near the main parking lot, one and three-fourths miles from the entrance gate. This was open to visitors during the summer for bathing, picnicking, sunning, and strolling at fees of twenty-five cents for each passenger car, twenty-five cents for each person, and ten cents for each child under twelve. The third part was designated a Nature Study Area, including Spermaceti Cove, a holly forest, and the entire side of the main drive north of the bay fishing section.

The largest area left for possible development as a State Park was the southerly portion of Island Beach in Ocean County. Most of this ten-mile finger of sand, less than a half-mile wide, was purchased in 1926 by Henry Phipps, who had made his fortune in steel as a Carnegie partner and who kept the property as he had found it. Phipps died in 1930, and the heirs continued his policy. In the early fifties, the Legislature provided a fund of two million seven hundred fifty thousand dollars for the purchase of wild-life preserves, particularly along the seacoast; and after considerable negotiation this section of Island Beach was procured by the State to be used mainly for public recreation.

This was opened to the public with certain restrictions, in 1959. The Park was divided into three areas. The upper three miles contained unusual examples of rare seacoast vegetation and was open to guided tours. Its beachfront, except during the summer season, could be used by surf fishermen. Lifeguards protected the one-

and-a-half-mile-long bathing area, and the five-mile lower tip of Island Beach, extending south to Barnegat Inlet, was preserved as a wild-life sanctuary open to surf fishermen and to guided tour service. Charges were made similar to those at Sandy Hook.

In 1963 an additional recreational area was in the process of development at the shore, a tract of about twenty-nine hundred acres at Corson's Inlet near Ocean City. This land is situated between the Garden State Parkway and the Intracoastal Waterway with three thousand feet of ocean frontage. Plans included facilities for picnicking and water sports, and part of the area was to be set aside as a bird refuge. Total cost of the park was estimated at nine hundred thousand dollars, of which the Federal Government's share would be two hundred seventy thousand dollars.

## In Wartimes

Two world conflicts in the twentieth century had repercussions in the social and economic life of the shore; World War II brought the greater upheaval. The influx of military personnel, the use of shore hotels as hospitals, the German submarine threat immediately offshore, the construction of new military bases—all these had widespread influence on the lives of the shore people.

During the first World War, Cape May County became a scene of much military activity. The Wissahickon Naval Training Barracks, an officers' training camp, and a naval air station were established at Cape May, and it was estimated that an average of fifteen thousand men were stationed in and around the resort. The regular summer visitors and cottagers were joined by the families and friends of the servicemen and the influx taxed Cape May's housing facilities. Every available room was occupied by officers and their families. The hotels made valiant efforts to care for all who sought accommodations, even putting cots in the halls. Local families entertained them and public affairs of all kinds offered additional recreation.

In Ocean County in 1914, just before the outbreak of war in Europe, a German company built what was at that time the most powerful radio station in the world, at Tuckerton on Osborn's Island, near the site of the massacre of Pulaski's troops during the Revolutionary War. A corresponding plant in Germany used the station to communicate with the United States after Germany was blockaded. The radio tower, 840 feet high, was the highest in existence at that time. It was alleged that information which led to the sinking of the *Lusitania* on May 7, 1915, was relayed from this station. When war was declared by the United States on April 6, 1917, the American Government took over the station and placed it in charge of the Navy. Marines and a naval detachment were located there during the war period. In the 1950's it was dismantled, and in the early 1960's the site became the "Mystic Islands," a real estate development with lagoon-front lots.

The most important development in Monmouth County was the establishment on May 16, 1917, about five weeks after American entry into the war, of Camp Alfred Vail as a Signal Corps center. It was constructed on the site of the old Monmouth racing park. Buildings and barracks were erected in May and June, and it received its first troops on July 9. During the ensuing months many thousands of men were sent there for training. On August 6, 1925, the post became Fort Monmouth in honor of its proximity to the site of one of the battles of the Revolutionary War.

The submarine menace off the Jersey shore during World War I was not as serious as in World War II, but a number of vessels were torpedoed by German U-boats. On one occasion residents of Long Beach heard heavy firing at sea and windows along the island shook and rattled. News was censored, but it was known locally that an American ship was sunk off Atlantic City and that a five-masted 2,440-ton schooner had been torpedoed off Cape May.

The northern section of the shore also noted the presence of U-boats, which sank coastwise vessels off Monmouth County. One U-boat was even brazen enough to shell Fort Hancock one summer evening. Shots from the vessel landed near the Coast Guard Station, but no damage was done. During the summer of 1918, U-boats attacked and sank tankers off the shore on two different occasions. Another sea tragedy took place off Seaside Park on August 17, when a Navy mine sweeper was mistaken at night for a submarine and sunk by an armed merchantman.

All the shore area was deeply involved in World War II activities. In Cape May County much of the pre-war and wartime effort centered around the Coast Guard Base established there after World War I, on the site of the naval training station. In 1940 Washington announced a naval air base was to be established at Cape May, and the Navy formally took over the Coast Guard air base; the Coast Guard unit was transferred to Cape May Point. In 1948 the Coast Guard resumed its control over the base. By 1952 an average of twelve hundred men were stationed there for training. The activities at the base brought new people and new families to the southern part of Cape May County.

Of wider significance was the Federal Government's taking over many Atlantic City hotels during the war. By 1943 the Army was occupying many of them, including the Traymore, the Breakers, the Brighton, the Shelburne, the St. Charles, the Dennis, the Chelsea, and the Arlington, with Air Corps trainees. In June, 1943, the Government leased Convention Hall for seventy-five thousand dollars a year. As facilities were constructed elsewhere for training the Air Corps men, plans were made in mid-1943 to give up the leases on a number of hotels. A few were to be retained for hospital purposes. The resort was then in a quandary over its immediate future. By August, however, 13 hotels had become convalescent hospitals, and by October many veterans began arriving at other hotels to await assignment to new programs. The average stay was two weeks, and the hotels served as rest centers. After V-J day there was a gradual decline in the use of the hotels by servicemen.

A more permanent influence was the establishment of the Atlantic City Naval Air Station at Pomona, between the Black Horse Pike and the White Horse Pike, just north of Pleasantville and Absecon. The base cost eight million dollars and included thirteen hundred acres of pine woods. The Navy took over the area in May, 1942, and hundreds of men and machines were brought in to construct buildings and runways. By mid-October, 1943, the Station was turning out pilots for the war fronts.

As part of the general demobilization program after the war, plans were made to lease parts of the base to domestic airlines, and Eastern Airlines signed an agreement for its use. Unsettled world conditions, however, led to the reinstatement of the air base in 1946, and it became a training center with personnel of two hundred officers and fourteen hundred men. After the outbreak of the Korean hostilities in 1950, facilities at the base were expanded and new accommodations were built for Navy personnel.

Changing times brought changing needs. In August, 1958, the Naval Air Station became the National Aviation Facilities Experimental Center, a part of the Federal Aviation Agency. This site was chosen because of its proximity to the high-density air traffic areas of New York, Philadelphia, and Washington, which offered an excellent environment for the "real life" study of air traffic control problems. Also, the Atlantic Ocean provided a vast, traffic-free, airspace over water for experimental flying. Its Measurement Range was used to collect scientific data on the performance of experimental equipment under actual flight conditions, including precision electronic and optical measuring and recording equipment. The latest types of computers were used to perform mathematical analyses of test data. The aircraft fleet stationed there included 20 representative types ranging from small single-engine aircraft to conventional multi-engine to the latest jet and turbo-prop aircraft. By 1962, personnel at the center totalled at least two thousand two hundred, including more than one thousand four hundred civilian employees and scores of officers.

The largest single military development at the shore during World War II was the expansion of Fort Monmouth near Eatontown and Long Branch. In July, 1935, the first radar work was done there, and as war seemed more imminent the signal training facilities were enlarged. By the fall of 1941 the Fort was the second largest military establishment in the State—Fort Dix was the largest. At that time the post was two miles long and housed approximately twelve thousand officers and men. By then a special Pigeon Breeding and Training Center was a part of the Signal Corps work. Following Pearl Harbor, a large construction program was undertaken. When increasing threats from the Soviet Union made the international situation tense in the late forties, facilities at Fort Monmouth were further expanded. By 1949, the local newspaper rightly called the post "the nerve center of the Signal Corps" and a "Major Cog in Shore Economy."

## SUBMARINES OFFSHORE

Submarine depredations during World War II reached serious proportions and brought intensive activity on the part of the Naval Air Patrol. Several German submarines were sunk by blimps from Lakehurst. In the summer of 1942, just north of Barnegat Inlet, a merchant ship was torpedoed and sunk in broad daylight within three miles of land. The submarine was then attacked by blimps, depth bombs were dropped, and soon patches of oil indicated a hit. In another instance, however, a Lakehurst blimp was shot down at sea in a gun battle with a U-boat. (The blimp was helium-filled and was able to make a landing on the sea.)

The sinking of tankers off the Jersey shore caused loss of life as well as of needed supplies of oil. Two stories of the experiences of seamen appeared in an Atlantic City paper five days apart in February, 1942. The Navy reported that on February 2 a Standard Oil tanker was torpedoed off New Jersey in daylight. Of the crew of 38 men, only three got ashore. The submarine hit the ship with one torpedo at 12:45 P.M., and then fired 17 shells into the sinking ship. It surfaced about two hundred yards from the lifeboats and looked them over carefully. "We saw eight or nine Germans on the conning tower," reported one of the survivors. The three survivors spent two days in a lifeboat in sub-zero weather.

Twelve men escaped when the *India Arrow* was torpedoed off the Jersey coast on February 7. The experience was described by one of them:

The tanker keeled over after the torpedoing and nine men were brought aboard my lifeboat. All looked alike, covered with oil. We drifted clear as the oil on the surface caught on fire. We were only about 300 feet from the tanker when the sub started to shell it. I could see the conning tower illuminated from the flaming surface of the sea. . . . We could hear the screams of the men in the water and their cries for help but we could not see them. . . . We could see the coast to the west and started toward there by oar. . . . It was tough going.

Flares were sent up from the lifeboats. Half a dozen ships were sighted by the men in the lifeboats, but they changed their courses at once to avoid any lurking submarine. The men then hoped that a patrol plane would rescue them, but none came. The next night they again sighted ships but could not attract their notice. Toward morning they sighted another boat in the fog and shot off two more flares. This boat, a fishing vessel, hove to and brought them ashore. The sinking brought the total number of vessels lost off the Atlantic coast between January 12 and February 12 up to 24.

Oil from the sunken tankers covered many beaches with thick black deposits. In June, 1942, six Monmouth County shore towns appealed to State and Federal authorities to help remove this oil scum. Several different experiments were made but only two methods seemed feasible: carting away or burying the deposit. (If it was dumped back into the sea it was only carried to some other beach.) It was learned that solidified oil and tar could be shoveled up and carted away and whatever traces were left could be buried. The State Highway Department provided a trench digger. Other debris brought in with the oil was burned.

As losses by submarines increased, it became evident that ships silhouetted against beachfront lights were easy prey for the U-boats. In March, 1942, the Army ordered a permanent coastal "dim-out." Lights along the beach were shaded to prevent the beams from showing on the seaward side, special blackout curtains were sold in the beach towns, and automobiles were not allowed to use full lights. By November of that year the submarine threat was more under control, and the Army ended the dim-out. This was superseded by a voluntary "brown out" to conserve electrical energy. Asbury Park made plans to take down its twenty thousand dollar dim-out screen along the boardwalk. Army and Navy authorities were quick to explain that should the submarine menace return, it would be necessary to adopt the special measures again, but this did not happen.

The end of the war in Europe caused no great rejoicing for everyone realized that the war was not ended. Bars did little business; in a few communities the schools closed in mid-morning and mill hands took the day off, but there was no real celebration. On V-J Day, however, the celebrating was noisy and widespread. The *Asbury Park Press* reported on August 15, 1945:

An exultant shore took a holiday today. . . . A few minutes after seven last night came the news of the Japanese surrender. . . . The celebration went on and on into the hours just before dawn. It was a night that will never be forgotten. . . . The siren went off at 7:05. . . . Confetti rained on the principal streets of Monmouth and Ocean County towns, fire signals shrieked hour after hour, impromptu motorcades playing a delirious accompaniment with horns and tin cans sped through every street. Hands were wrung until arms ached. . . . Kisses were free.

The shore survived the pressures of two World Wars without permanent economic dislocations, and in 1945 the future looked peaceful. Within five years, however, the Korean crisis caused further expansion of military installations in the four shore counties.

One post-war development was the motel whose colorful construction changed the face of Atlantic City, and to a lesser extent the other large resorts. The motel provided a new source of competition to the large hostelries along the Boardwalk. The first was built outside the boundaries of Atlantic City; a city ordinance prohibited their construction inside the city limits. In 1953, however, the ruling was changed to permit them within the city and on the Boardwalk. From 1954 to 1962, 73 motels, or "motor inns" as some operators preferred to call them, were built in Atlantic City. Many of them were four and five stories high, and some were equipped with "efficiency apartments." Most of them provided swimming pools and some offered ice rinks for the entertainment of their guests. Old hotels and guest houses were torn down to make room for the new type of structure and its essential parking facilities. Colored all shades from startling chartreuse to skyblue pink, the motel offered a new and popular type of resort accommodation.

### SHORE CONSERVATION

Another problem, more fundamental than the temporary economic dislocation caused by war or motels, was the constantly recurring menace of beach erosion. The most important asset of the shore is the coastline. On this main attraction the shorefront recreation industry was based, and the beaches were dependent upon deposits of sand left there by the littoral drift of currents. Without the availability and stability of beaches, no shorefront recreation could continue to prosper. It was evident that narrow, unusable beaches and damaged, precariously-pitched dwellings and boardwalks were detrimental to business. An examination of any eroded beachfront proved the direct relationship between progressive beach erosion and gradual beach abandonment by the public.

During the establishment of the various resorts along the coast, sand dunes had been leveled and the supply of sand to the beaches correspondingly diminished. During periodic storms, portions of the shorefront were washed away. The erosion processes often undermined physical properties. The oceanfront from Sandy Hook to Cape May, as charted by the Federal Coast and Geodetic Survey over a period of many decades, showed the erosion of some beaches and accretions on others, but on the whole there had been a small net loss each year. In some of the places surveyed this loss had averaged more than six feet a year.

Some locations were particularly subject to erosion. At Cape May, for instance, the old whaling village of Town Bank gradually was washed completely away. Long Branch in the northern section of the shore began to feel the effects of erosion severely by the later nineteenth century. Ocean Avenue has been rebuilt three times since 1862. Each time it was moved farther inland as the ocean continued to encroach.

Gradually civic authorities began to realize the need for protective measures such as sand-tight jetties, sea walls, groins, and breakwaters, all of which represented major capital expenditures, requiring State, county, and local cooperation. The first State aid was forthcoming in 1920 when the Legislature appropriated two hundred fifty thousand dollars to aid the beach municipalities in erosion control. Other appropriations followed, and more jetties and other controls were constructed with funds matched by local governments and some county contributions. In 1944, the Legislature passed a law permitting grants-in-aid to municipalities undertaking definite coast-protection projects. The localities were eligible for the allotment of State funds up to one-half the construction costs. In the year ending June 30, 1947, eleven projects from Sea Bright south to Cape May involved a total outlay of $1,417,976, of which $852,297 was paid by the State.

There was considerable discussion over what materials should be used in the projects. It was generally agreed that despite the greater expense stone was best. On the eleven projects just mentioned, approximately 314,000 tons of stone were employed. Some municipalities had earlier built simple jetties of creosoted timber and steel sheet piling, with creosoted timber planking and master piles. However, normal deterioration, coupled with battering storms, and, in the case of steel, abrasion by sand, made the life of this type of construction uncertain. Later the envelopment of the timber and steel jetties with large quarry stone was tried with fair results. Finally the decision was made to recommend jetty construction of quarry stone only.

In addition to the efforts of the State, the shore localities themselves made determined attempts to prevent the loss of their beaches. At Ocean City, for instance, groins and stone jetties were constructed, and by 1948 a three-thousand-foot jetty extending into Great Egg Harbor Inlet at the entrance of the channel was finished. However, more construction was necessary as other sections of Ocean City's beach continued to wear away. In 1952 engineers recommended the lengthening of the existing stone jetties along the beach, at a total estimated cost of $1,882,000, and urged artificial beach reclamation by hydraulic sand pumping.

Atlantic County faced the problem of erosion in the nineteenth century. Between 1880 and 1910 Longport lost 184 acres of beach, and its first sea wall was breached by storms. In 1918 the resort built another sea wall and a series of jetties, which aided in preserving the shoreline. Margate, the resort north of Longport, constructed its first jetties in 1924, and Ventnor followed. The largest amount of conservation work was centered at Atlantic City. Following the big storms of the 1940's new protective barriers were built. In 1950 the resort completed five timber-groins of upright piling, some of which extended approximately six hundred feet seaward, and the same year riprapping at the Inlet was finished by the placing of nearly eight thousand tons of stone on the ocean side of the bulkhead. In 1951 the local paper announced that two million two hundred thousand dollars had been expended in the Atlantic City area during the previous six years in the fight against erosion. This amount included funds from the city, the county, and the State.

Some of the resorts in Monmouth County conducted a continuous struggle against the washing away of the beaches. Much of the work centered at Long Branch, although Asbury Park, Ocean Grove, and other resorts built protective jetties, bulkheads, sea walls, and groins. In the 1930's 13 steel and rock jetties were constructed at Long Branch, protecting most of the beach area as far south as the Deal borough line. The sea wall at Sea Bright proved effective in the hurricane of 1950.

The expense of building jetties presented a serious problem. Long Branch became financially pressed in its endeavor to retain its beach front of four and a half miles. Between 1937 and 1949 it issued $1,373,324 in bonds as its share toward the construction of jetties and bulkheads. The devastation caused by the 1944 hurricane showed the need for an extensive building program. Twenty-three jetties were built between 1946 and 1949, at a cost of $1,090,000. Of this sum the city contributed $570,000; the State, $400,000; and the county, $120,000.

### STORM

In the spring of 1962, the New Jersey seashore was battered by the worst storm in its history. On March 6 and 7, new-moon tides were driven landward by gale-force winds that originated in a high pressure area about three hundred miles off Cape Cod and that blew for six hundred miles toward a low pressure area centered off Cape Hatteras. At this point, two dangerous conditions existed: abnormally high tides and strong northeast winds. Within a few hours millions of tons of water piled up on the New Jersey beaches. The effect was more devastating because the winds ranged up to sixty miles an hour and continued for many hours, sweeping across a wide expanse of ocean before striking the shore. Waves as high as twenty feet sent great quantities of water surging against the shore, piling blow on blow. Flood conditions continued even after the winds began to die down because it took so long a time for the mass of water to flow back from the shore. Moreover, winds and floods caused pyramiding damage; as houses washed away, they crashed into other structures still standing which in turn gave away and rammed still others.

Most of the sea islands were inundated, loss of life was considerable, and damage mounted into the millions. Mainland authorities strove to send relief as news of the destruction trickled through from the shore. Graphic accounts of the losses appeared in metropolitan papers.

We were flying over Surf City, one correspondent wrote on Tuesday, March 7. . . . As far as we could see, both north and south, all of Long Beach Island was under water. We turned south over a sea of muddy water out of which stuck telephone poles, leaning askew, and heading to what seemed nowhere. Window frames, tables, chairs, boards, and all manner of other debris floated in this sea. Waves were tossing over the island into Little Egg Harbor, and washing back into the sea. The sea had the whole island under its surf.

Year-round residents who had not had time to evacuate found themselves undergoing harrowing experiences. One elderly man, living at Landis Avenue and Thirty-Seventh Street, Sea Isle City, described the night of March 7:

Five houses near us were blown or washed down. Some floated into our back yard tearing down the fence. All night long we could hear them banging into our house. The water was seeping into our living room; about three feet of it covered the floor. We could hear the crash of waves against the house, and nearby buildings falling. One house on the corner that had been standing fifty years went down with a terrific crash. My wife and I went up to the attic and lay on the bare floor all Tuesday night, praying.

During the summer of 1962, shore communities, aided by county, State, and Federal funds, embarked on a massive rehabilitation program, with forty million dollars to provide emergency repairs and make a start on permanent beach protection. Millions of tons of sand were pumped or bulldozed onto the beaches. In the spring of 1963 the Mayor of Beach Haven reported two hundred sixty thousand cubic yards of it had been pumped onto one and a half miles of beach and that fourteen thousand discarded Christmas trees had been buried to strengthen the rebuilt dunes; the Mayor of Long Beach Township said that over a million cubic yards had been added to the beach there. Other major public projects completed included multi-million-dollar sea walls, dunes, and bulkheads at Ocean City, Stone Harbor, Sea Isle City, Cape May, Long Branch, and Sea Bright; almost a million had been spent at Harvey Cedars on sewage and water systems; three hundred thousand dollars on beach fill at Ocean City, nine hundred fifty thousand dollars on a dune and beach fill at Brigantine, four hundred fifty thousand dollars for the same at Absecon Inlet in Atlantic City, three hundred thousand dollars for pumping sand at Middletown Township, and the same for jetties at Barnegat Inlet and more than three million dollars on Long Beach Island.

The recovery was remarkable. Visitors were amazed at the amount of rehabilitation within the year. In Ocean City scarcely any trace of the storm remained. The Mayor declared to one reporter in the spring of 1963, "All homes have been rebuilt. . . . Some have put their homes on higher pilings. The more courageous . . . rebuilt on the same foundations." New bulkheads of wood and stone had been constructed along the beach from Thirty-fourth to Fifty-seventh Streets, the scene of the worst damage. The Mayor of Sea Isle City, where 285 homes were lost, thanked the Corps of Engineers for the "beautiful beach." A new promenade with a sea wall top paved with bituminous asphalt replaced the boardwalk. As for the people, he said, "One storm, even like the one we had, won't chase them out." At Cape May, a permanent bulkhead was put in. This was a sea wall of concrete and rock extending along its two and a half miles of beachfront. On the land side the wall stood from three and a half to four and a half feet above the street level; facing the ocean was a stone wall a foot higher than the promenade. Even at Harvey Cedars, almost washed away as a town, with 39 houses taken by the sea and 90 badly damaged, the Mayor reported that 19 houses had been replaced, most of them on the sand dunes from which they had vanished. "People have a respect for the water," he said, "but no fear of it." Most of them, he admitted, were rebuilding their houses on pilings 12 to 20 feet high; they were formerly four to six feet high.

However, some sections of beach, noticeably at Cape May, Avalon, Sea Isle City, and Ocean City, had washed away for good, and in these areas retrenchment from the sea occurred. Large gaps could still be observed where buildings had once stood, particularly at Harvey Cedars, Strathmere, West Wildwood, Avalon, Surf City, and Sea Isle City. Moreover, the new protective devices were considered insufficient to secure many shore properties from damage should a similar storm strike the coast again. Adequate long-range protection would require the expenditure of many more millions of dollars. Nevertheless, despite the damage done, it was estimated in the fall of 1962 that the coastal area had done a $1,068,000,000 summer business, which was two percent more than that of the year before.

The shore recreation business is still the biggest industry in New Jersey. The sun and the sea will always draw vacationers. Other storms may strike the coast, but people will continue to find the area attractive. "Sea-bathing" will still stir "the torpid liver" and "scatter tingling sensations of pleasure over the frame." The surf will still "lubricate the joints like oil" and "grave men" will still "fling out their limbs like colts in pasture . . . (and) dignified women . . . sport like girls at recess." New Jersey is a State greatly blessed with the gift of a seashore to provide so many people with so much pleasure.

# BIBLIOGRAPHICAL NOTES

No attempt has been made to provide documentation for the statements made in this book. For full footnotes, the reader is referred to the copious collection in the author's 1953 two-volume edition, *The Jersey Shore,* available in many of the larger libraries. However, it was believed advisable to include in this monograph suggestions concerning the more valuable works and newspapers. Most helpful repositories were the Stewart Collection of New Jerseyana in the Glassboro State College Library, the State Library in Trenton, the State Historical Society Library in Newark, and the libraries of the County Historical Societies.

For primary sources, of special value were the files of the *Asbury Park Press,* Asbury Park Press Building; of the *National Standard and Salem County Adviser,* in the County Clerk's Office, Salem; of the *Woodbury Constitution,* Gloucester County Historical Society Library, Woodbury; Thomas Gordon, *A Gazetteer of the State of New Jersey* (Trenton, 1834), in Stewart Collection, Glassboro State College; Lawrence Furlong, *American Coast Pilot* (Newburyport, Massachusetts, 1804, first edition, 1796), in the library of Mr. L. B. Newcomb, Glen Lake Avenue, Pitman, New Jersey; *Journal of Robert Juet,* crew member of Henry Hudson's ship; Barber and Howe, *Historical Collections of New Jersey* (1842 edition at Glassboro); Bishop Francis Asbury Journal quoted in Edwin Salter and George Beekman, *Old Times in Old Monmouth* (Freehold, 1887); Spicer Journal quoted in Lewis Stevens, *History of Cape May*

*County* (Cape May, 1897); Beesley, *Geology of the County of Cape May* (1857), quoted in Cornelius Weygandt, *Down Jersey* (New York, 1940); *New Jersey Archives*, especially references to whaling industry; *Journal of Thomas Hopkins,* saltmaker of Great Egg Harbor, printed in *Pennsylvania Magazine of History and Biography,* Volume XLII (1918) [the manuscript is in Library of Pennsylvania Historical Society, Philadelphia]; John F. Watkins, *Annals of Philadelphia and Pennsylvania* (Philadelphia, 1857), in Stewart Collection, Glassboro, containing good descriptions of trips to the Jersey Shore, early 19th Century; reminiscences of Uriah Norcross, then 88 years old, in 1927, published in *Atlantic City Evening Union,* August 2, 1927, in Heston Scrapbook in Atlantic City Library; *Compendium of Censuses, 1726–1905* (Trenton, 1906); Gustav Kobbé, *The Jersey Coast and Pines* (Short Hills, 1889), interesting guidebook; Dr. J. F. Leaming, "The Beach Party," 1835, in *Cape May County Gazette* (March 24, 1933); Emma B. Aldrich, ms., journal of recollections, in Cape May County Historical Society Library; Allen Brown, *The Character and Employment of the Early Settlers on the Seacoast of New Jersey* (Newark, 1879); G. A. Raybold, *Reminiscences of Methodism in West Jersey* (New York, 1849); *New Jersey Historical Records Survey,* Works Progress Administration; Reuben Willets, ms., journal in Cape May County Historical Society Library; Professor George Cook papers in Rutgers University Library; *Apprenticeship Records,* Township Book of Great Egg Harbor, quoted in Frank Stewart, *Notes on Old Gloucester County,* Volume I; Emily Bennett file of newspaper clippings, in Cape May County Historical Society Library; *Freehold Transcript,* in Monmouth County Historical Society Library. [see especially Mrs. Richardson's recollections of 1845, written in 1895 and in *Transcript,* June 17, 1927]; *West Jersey Press* clippings (1876), in Cooper Scrapbook in Camden County Historical Society Library, Camden; *Summer Days in New Jersey* (1885), contemporary description, pamphlet in Pennsylvania

Historical Society Library, Philadelphia; sign for the Mansion House, 1839, Cape May [sign is in Cape May County Historical Society Museum, Cape May Court House]; T. R. Rose and H. G. Woolman, *Historical Atlas of the New Jersey Coast* (Philadelphia, 1878), steel engraving source for illustrations, in Stewart Collection, Glassboro; Alfred Cooper, *My Traditions and Memories, 1859-1938* (Cape May Court House, 1938) in author's private library; *Proceedings of the New Jersey Historical Society;* William C. Ulyat, *Life at the Sea-Shore* (Princeton, New Jersey, 1880), contemporary description, pamphlet, in Pennsylvania Historical Society Library, Philadelphia; Francis B. Lee, *Scrapbooks,* in Cape May County Historical Society Library, Cape May Court House, newspaper clippings; *Achievements by the Sea* (Ocean Grove, 1881), pamphlet in Pennsylvania Historical Society Library, Philadelphia; Silas Morse Scrapbook, Atlantic County Historical Society Library, Somers Point, clippings and pictures; *New Jersey Songs and Music, 1849-1926,* portfolio in Princeton University Library; John B. Smith, "The New Jersey Salt Marsh and Its Improvement," New Jersey Experimental Station, Bulletin No. 207 (1907); George Cook, *Report of the State Geologist, 1872;* Cora June Sheppard, Shiloh, New Jersey, scrapbooks of newspaper clippings; *Atlantic Review* (Atlantic City), early 20th Century, Somers Point Library of Atlantic County Historical Society; *Matawan Journal,* clippings in Freehold Library of Monmouth County Historical Society; Department of Conservation and Economic Development, *Annual Reports.*

Many secondary sources were consulted in the collection of material. Most of these can be found in the Stewart Collection of New Jerseyana at Glassboro State College or in the State Library at Trenton. Most of them are not up to date. Of particular importance were regional and state histories, especially those by William Nelson, *The New Jersey Coast in Three Centuries* (New York, 1902), and Alfred Heston, *South Jersey,* two volumes, (New York, 1930); Alfred Heston, *Jersey Waggon Jaunts,* two volumes, (Camden, 1926); Francis B. Lee, *New Jersey as a Colony and as a State,* four volumes, (New York, 1902); William Starr Myers, *The Story of New Jersey* (New York, 1944); Alfred Heston, *Absegami Annals* (Camden, 1904); Irving Kull, *New Jersey, A History,* four volumes, (New York, 1930). Also helpful were the voluminous county histories, mostly written in the 19th century, including Franklin Ellis, *History of Monmouth County* (Freehold, 1885); Lewis Stevens, *History of Cape May County* (Cape May, 1897); William Fischer, *Biographical Cyclopaedia of Ocean County, New Jersey* (Philadelphia, 1899); John F. Hall, *Daily Union History of Atlantic City and County* (Atlantic City, 1900); Edwin Salter and George Beekman, *Old Times in Old Monmouth* (Freehold, 1887); Edwin Salter, *History of Monmouth and Ocean Counties* (Bayonne, 1890). A number of local histories were real aids in the search for material, particularly Leah Blackman, *History of Little Egg Harbor Township, Burlington County, New Jersey* (Camden, 1880); Morris Daniels, *The Story of Ocean Grove* (New York, 1919); E. H. Stokes, *Ocean Grove, Its Origins and Progress* (Philadelphia, 1874); Works Progress Administration Historical Writing Project, *Entertaining a Nation, the Story of Long Branch* (Long Branch, 1940); Charles Nash, *The Lure of Long Beach* (Long Beach, 1936); Cornelius Weygandt, *Down Jersey* (New York, 1940); Dorothy Cross, *The Archeology of New Jersey* (Trenton, 1941); Charles Philhower, *Indian Lore of New Jersey* (n. d. pamphlet); Wheaton Lane, *From Indian Trail to Iron Horse* (Princeton, 1940); K. Braddock-Rogers, "Salt Works of New Jersey during the American Revolution," in *Journal of Chemical Education,* Volume XV (December, 1938); Leonard Lundin, *New Jersey, Cockpit of the Revolution* (Princeton, 1940); John Clement, "Atlantic County, Then and Now," *Proceedings of the Surveyors' Association of West New Jersey* (Camden, 1880); Laura L. T. Willis, *Early History of Atlantic County* (Kutztown, Pennsylvania, 1915); Witmer Stone, *The Plants of*

*Southern New Jersey, Annual Report of State Museum* (Trenton, 1911); Frank Butler, *History of Southern New Jersey* (pamphlet, clippings from Atlantic City Press, 1949); Albert Hand, *A Book of Cape May;* and Thomas A. Leonard, *From Indian Trail to Electric Rail* (Atlantic Highlands, New Jersey, 1923).

# INDEX